The Love Factor
Truths to Explore Before You Say, "I Do".

Dr. Daniel J. Vassell Sr.
and
Jennifer Ann-Marie Vassell

Foreword by Dr. R. Lamar Vest

©2019 Dr. Daniel J. Vassell Sr & Jennifer Ann-Marie Vassell

All rights reserved. This book or any portion thereof may not be reproduced or used in any manner whatsoever without the express written permission of the publisher except for the use of brief quotations in a book review.

ISBN: 978-1-7322962-9-9

Endorsements

Engaged couples entering into a marriage relationship often under-value premarital counseling and they often underestimate the tools and commitment needed to protect and preserve the marriage relationship. Dr. Vassell and his wife Jenny utilize their successful relationship as a foundation to help prepare others to understand the sanctity of marriage. They provide Biblical and deeply passionate guidance in this must-read book, The Love Factor in Marriage: Explore What You Need to Know Before You Say, "I Do".

—Dr. Jimmy Harper
Chapel Pastor
Lee University
Cleveland, TN

Dr. Daniel and Jenny Vassell share their wealth of experience and knowledge on marriage and relationships in their latest book. There are many things to consider before you say, "I do." The Vassells share the keys to a long, loving, relationship. I would recommend this book as required reading to anyone who is planning on getting married.

—Bishop Gary Lewis
Administrative Bishop
Church of God
South Georgia

The names Daniel and Jenny conjure up sterling memories of being dynamic orators on the frontline subject of love and marriage. Endorsing this book is such a pleasure as the authors— prolific and real—expound the scriptural and fundamental issue that needs bold, uncompromising exposure.

The exhausting research and open heartedly frank discussion uncovers the passionate convictions of a warm "couple." A more straight devoted and deep talk is difficult to find.

May this thoroughly researched and professionally presented idea offer solace to a loveless society and reignite love in marriage. The promulgation of family values in society is urgent. Please read on and promote.

—Emmanuel Joseph Moodley
Senior Pastor,
Bethsaida International Ministries
Durban, South Africa

The Love Factor in Marriage Explored! What You Need to Know Before You Say, "I Do" has been written with great concern for today's young adults, marriages and families. Dr. Daniel and Jenny Vassell have written with a burden to see marriages and families come under the rule of God's love. With caring insight, the authors have presented from their years of experience ministering couples and families and expressing the need to follow the rule of God's love in the home.

—Dr. Oliver McMahan
Dean of Ministries
Church of God Theological Seminary
Cleveland, TN

Dr. Daniel and Jenny Vassell are an example of those who has learned the meaning of unconditional love. They have shown their love through their relationship together and also with James, Aleah, his God, and his church. Based on this background, I have looked forward to the completion of *The Love Factor in Marriage Explored! What You Need to Know Before You Say, "I Do."* You will enjoy this book.

—Dr. G. Dennis McGuire
Former General Overseer
Church of God International Offices
Cleveland, TN

Dr. Daniel and Jenny Vassell have hearts for God and for the church. However, their zeal for spiritual things does not surpass Daniel's zeal for his family. It is evident that he understands that his relationship with his wife will greatly impact his relationship with his children, as well as with God. They are dedicated students and have worked diligently to prepare a manuscript to relate Daniel's findings regarding the establishment of a Godly foundation of love in couples and family relationships. I commend them for their effort to influence a society full of dysfunctional marriages and families.

We must help the church realize that before the church was instituted, God created the family. Now, we must do all we can to save it!

—John D. Childers
Secretary General
Church of God
Cleveland, TN

The Love Factor in Marriage Explored! What You Need to Know Before You Say, "I Do" can help you and your expected spouse beat the odds of divorce and master the essential principles that make a successful marriage. This is an excellent resource for young adults and pastors to use as a premarital resource.

—Dr. John T. Ramos
Former, Doctor of Ministry in Marriage and Family
Professor
Cleveland, TN

Dr. Daniel and Jenny Vassell's *The Love Factor in Marriage Explored! What You Need to Know Before You Say, "I Do"* communicates that Jesus' love for the church is the pattern God set for marital love relationships. This book challenges husbands to love their lives as co-labors and equal partners, to recognize them as "gifts," not as possessions. The indwelling presence of God will supply the needed love for all couples to find complete fulfillment and happiness in marriage and repair any broken pieces of your relationship regardless of circumstances. Not just another book on marriage, this has practical ideas for expanding the love factor in your marriage when you get married.

—Dr. Daniel Boling
Former Administrative Bishop
Church of God
West Virginia

In a day when marriage is under attack, Daniel and Jenny Vassell offer their hearts in addressing the foundation of the Biblical marital relationship. The Love Factor in Marriage reasserts a biblical view of love and thereby reminds all of us of its power to restore and renew marriage.

—John Kie Vining, D. Min.
International Director of Family Ministry
Cleveland, TN

Dr. Daniel and Jenny Vassell have brought to focus an up-to-date 21st century freshness of the love principle that is so vital in the marital affinity. *The Love Factor in Marriage* does raise one's consciousness. The provocative thought principles, ideas, and practicalities are worth being inwardly digested and demonstrated.

He etymologized the word love, and vividly declares that "love is knowledge, service, and commitment." The affirmation of women can be clearly envisioned as a positive note, while from a negative perspective, abuse/bullying is "love's buster."

If anyone wants the rewards of love, try his suggested lists of ways a husband and wife can express love to one another.

—Dr. Quan L. Miller
Senior Pastor, 910 Church of God
Orlando, Florida

The biblical injunction, "Husbands, love your wives," is set forth in the text in the most serious manner. It is compared with the relationship between Christ and the church. However, this advice is often slighted because of a lack of careful reflection. In *The Love Factor in Marriage Explored! What You Need to Know Before You Say, "I Do,"* Dr. Daniel and Jenny Vassell have gently, but firmly, reminded us that God has created us with the ability to love and the capacity to be loved. Consequently, we have an obligation to love our partners, and in so doing we achieve our full potential according to God's design. *The Love Factor in Marriage Explored! What You Need to Know Before You Say, "I Do"* is a must read for all prospected married couples.

—Bishop Wayne A. Vernon
Senior Pastor, West Toronto Church of God
Toronto, Canada

Table of Contents

Dedication xiii

Foreword xv

Preface xvii

Introduction xix

Acknowledgements xxi

Chapters
1. Chaste Love 25
2. The Modes of Love 43
3. Complimentary Love 65
4. Loving Who I am 77
5. Submitted Lovers 91
6. Companionship Lovers 105
7. Love's Grandeur 109
8. Love Busters 113
9. Premarital Discussions 127
10. The Forever Love 151

Dedication

This book is dedicated to my parents, Evangelist William and Louise Vassell, who loved and were faithful to each other during more than 45 year of marriage. Their lives exemplified the true Biblical love—unconditional *agape* love—for one another during difficult times and as well as happy times.

It is also dedicated to my loving, lovely wife and co-author of this book, Jenny, for her patience and love during our years of marriage. She has, through love and grace, given me time to learn how to love her, as Christ requires. Wow, you bring the best out of me.

It is dedicated to my son, Daniel James Vassell Jr., who has made us proud parents and is following in his parents foot steps. He is a graduate of Lee with a B.A. in Theology and a MA in Mental Health counseling and is now an ordained minister of the Church of God and an anointed minister of music and a Mental Health counselor in Chattanooga, TN.

Finally, it is also, dedicated to our lovely daughter, Jennifer Aleah Ann Vassell, who has now graduated from Samford University with a B.F.A. in Musical Theatre and is now performing all over North America and sharing the gospel of Christ through her unique stage.

Foreword

We live in a rapidly changing world. The speed at which our world is changing catches many of us completely off guard, until some revelation or incident reveals how far off course we've gotten. Many are frightened by these changing times and retreat into the comfort of past traditions and mind-sets. Others feel threatened by the change in the status quo and resist any change at all. Unfortunately, the changes caused by the explosion of communication, technology, and knowledge have affected the family, in general, and marital relationships, in particular.

However, in the midst of this change, there are some absolutes. Dr. Daniel and Jenny Vassell have identified one of these absolutes in writing, *The Love Factor in Marriage Explored! Thing that You Need to Know Before You Say, "I Do."* After years of ministry to singles and couples, their burdens for young adults, marriages and the marital relationship have prompted them to once again call Christians to love their spouses as the Bible demands. Writing primarily from the Ephesians 5:25 perspective, Daniel and Jenny insist that husbands and wives should not let their love for each other be determined by what Hollywood portrays or by the actions of those in contemporary society. There is clear biblical instruction regarding how a husband and wife ought to treat each other.

The Love Factor in Marriage Explored! What You Need to Know Before You Say, "I Do" can serve as a valuable resource to pastors, engaged couples, and singles who are anticipating marriage. It gives clear biblical instruction, valuable insight, and practical suggestions for keeping love the vital factor in the marital relationship.

—Dr. R. Lamar Vest
(Former) International Presiding Bishop, Church of God,
(Former) President of the American Bibles Society
(Former) President of Pentecostal Theology Seminary
Cleveland, TN

Preface

In 1998, my pastor, Bishop Devon Dixon invited me to speak during the church's family month of November. I sought God for a word, and He gave me the text from Ephesians. As I prepared the sermon, I realized that what the Lord was revealing to me would take much more than a 40-minute sermon to convey His message to the church about marriage. The brethren who heard the message encouraged me to do more research on the topic, and because of my findings, *The Love Factor In Marriage* series began.

Summing up all that is involved with fulfilling the command given by God to love one's wife and for the wife to respect her own husband, is difficult to put into a single volume.

I do not pretend to have all the answers; however, I pray that this text will raise the consciousness of every reader, thus, allowing the Holy Spirit to minister in a way that will ultimately bring about concerted reform.

As you read this book, I pray that the Holy Spirit will minister to you as He did to me. May *The Love Factor in Marriage Explored, What You Need to Know Before You say, "I Do,"* help young adults and pre-married couples successfully face and survive the 21st century with God as the head of their relationship and ultimately families.

Introduction

When I began writing the first Love Factor in Marriage book, I wanted to present a resource material that would be beneficial to those couples that are experiencing difficulties in their marriages.

I researched many different areas that could affect married couples. I learned that there is a lot of abuse and a lot of single-parent families. I learned that many marriages are in trouble because they do not create a community of love.

When individuals look at the events that are taking place around them such as terrorism, wars, natural disasters, economical unrest and the constant pressures that many couples are facing; many tend to get nervous and wonder if it makes sense to get married. On the contrary these events should support the need to have loving community support. After all, what is better than a loving marriage? With so much anxiety in the world, families need each other for comfort and support; it is easy for marriages to crumble if God is not at the helm.

God has given us guidelines for good marriage relationships. His Word is the main adhesive that will hold marriages together. We must follow His direction, depend on Him, and ask for His leadership daily so we can have Godly marriages; marriages that stand the test of time. The guidelines for building a successful marriage come through proper education and training; much of which can be provided through proper premarital counseling.

In order for a marriage to stand that test of time, the Bible says, "*'...a Man will leave his father and mother and be joined to his wife, and the two will become one flesh.' This is a great mystery, and I am applying it to Christ and the church. Each of you, however, should love his wife as himself, and a wife should respect her husband* (Ephesians 5:31-33)."

Acknowledgments

Many people have assisted me in preparing the first *Love Factor in Marriage* book. They helped me lay the foundation, so credit is still due to them.

I would like to express appreciation to my pastor, the Bishop Devon A. Dixon Sr., his lovely wife and ministry companion, Heather, and the members of the East Chester Church of God family in Bronx, New York, for their encouragement.

Appreciation is extended to Sonia Stone and Shandrika Languely, personal friends, for their help and encouragement in the early draft.

Thanks to Rev. Joycelyn Brown—who was youth pastor of Driftwood Church of God and an English teacher in Toronto, Canada—for reading the book to see if it addressed the issue of love between husbands and wives and its relationship to youth and children.

The Reverend Bishop Cauldric Alex, pastor of Cambria Church of God in Boston, Massachusetts—a personal friend and student of the Word—for his help and insights on the abuse of women in the 20th century.

Dr. Yvonne Johnson—wife of Father, Dr. Raphael Johnson, the senior pastor of Holy Trinity Parish Church in Cambria Heights, New York. Dr. Yvonne Johnson is professor of English at Columbia University in New York, New York, and she read the manuscript for readability.

A special thanks to Mardene Carr for her excellent research and contribution with the writing, editing, marketing and all the background work to launch this project. You were our right hand; we appreciate your talent, gifts and the time you spent helping us all throughout the journey.

Special thanks to our brother and graphic art designer Wesley Thomas of Cape Town, South Africa, *www.wettrock.co.za* and email *info@wettrock.co.za* for relaying the cover graphic art and for the other promotional package he offered us.

I also want to thank another family and preacher friend of ours, Bishop Ronnie and Sherrie Reid for their advice and encouragement to write a *Love Factor* for their young daughters.

Last, but not least, very special thanks to my daughter and critique Jennifer Aleah Ann Vassell for her insight, revelation and encouragement. Upon reading and hearing me preach the contents of *The Love Factor in Marriage*, around the age of 13-14 she told me, "Dad, you must write a Love Factor book for young adults and teenagers." The book became a reality because of her.

Finally, I want to thank God for my loving wife Jenny, for joining me by adding her insight, knowledge and wisdom to this book. For years we have traveled and conducted Marriage and Family conferences, but she did not want to write. However, because of her love for the young adults in our culture, she laid aside her fears and joined me on this writing project.

Whatever the result of this book may be, I give credit to all who offered suggestions, insights and prayers. If reading this book impacts one life, or one million lives, their help will have been rewarded.

Acknowledgements

I especially give honor and praise to God for His guidance, His Word, and His love. Without Him this book would not have been possible.

Chapter 1

Chaste Love

Whether you have grown up in the church for most of your life, or you just became a Christian, let me ask you, "If you should find Mr. or Mrs. Right today and get married, would you know the kind of marriage and family you want? Would it be like your mother and father? Would be like Rebecca and Isaac; Sarah and Abraham or one of your lifetime heroes or celebrities? Would it be like your faithful grandparents? Who would it be like?" You may not have the perfect couple that you would like to pattern your marriage off, but do not be like many couples who got married without counting the cost.

Begin your relationship journey by choosing to practice being a chaste lover… A chaste lover is one who is a pure, modest, decent and practices living a life governed by the word and Spirit of God; rather than practicing a relationship governed by the culture of the day.

Chaste lovers are young adults and pre-married Christian couples that are looking forward to having a life full of the favor of God in their marriage. A chaste lover's relationship is one free from all of what is lustful or scandalous to a wholesome relationship. A chaste love is primarily referring to a godly pre- married couple's relationship that is refraining from all acts or even thoughts or desires that are not becoming for the child of God until they say their marriage vows.

Sure, no married couple is perfect, and hence there is no marriage that can be perfect. However, if you start your marriage with the right chaste lover, and receive the proper supports, then that marriage can be as close to perfect as possible. Jeff Herring, a relationship coach and expert, in an article entitled, *Marriage: 4 Kinds of Marriage Mate* said, "Marriage is one the biggest challenges a person will ever face in life." Herring says, "Everyone wants a soul mate, and many times relationships will start out that way. Eventually however cracks become visible as the years of exposure to the elements begin to take a toll. Over time, the relationships degenerations and couples drift from being soul mates into being other kind of mates." As children of God, should we marry our soul mates or our companions? (Genesis 2:18). Herring went on to say, there are four kinds of marriage mates: soul mates, life mates, roommates and cell mates.

He describes soul mates as couples in a marriage who feel connected at a soul-ullar level, where strong connection and passion is high. Life Mates have simply decided to spend their lives together, even though some of the passion and luster have worn off. These couples genuinely love each other and care about each other; they are just not passionately in love. The Room Mates are couples who have drifted from soul mates into roommates. The drift is not fast or intentional, that's why it is called a drift. Couples get along like roommates do, with some friendliness and no passion.

Herring states that Cell Mates are the worst kind of relationship. These couples feel trapped in a situation that neither of them believes they can get out of. People settle for less and stay in a loveless and painful situation. They intend to maintain their "till death do us part" vows, hoping the other goes first.

According to the above descriptions, which kind of mate would you want to be? I believe most readers would say the soul-mate. Good choice, but how do you plan to achieve a soul-mate kind of marriage?

Fruit-Mate

Elohim, the creator of marriage, said, "It is not good for the man to be [*alone*], I will make a helper suitable for him" (Gen. 2:18). Elohim made Adam a suitable female companion with whom he could share a lifetime of commitment, intimacy, and passion. Without Eve, Adam was without an intimate partner to share his life with. The coming of Eve into the marriage fulfilled the missing portion of the equation that God designed so that Adam could experience love, passion, intimacy, pleasure, and procreation. God designed Adam the man, and Eve the woman, to live in love, intimacy, passion, and commitment as a model for all humanity.

When God created the first couple, He set up the principle for marriage and I believe God made the first couple to live at what Herring call, the soul-**mate, however, I would prefer to call it the "Fruit-Mate"**.

In Genesis 1:26-28, He (God – Elohim) blessed them (Adam and Eve) and gave them three basic commands to live by in their marriage; these commands for marriage have not changed. Sin has made a havoc of the commands, but good news, the Holy Spirit has come to restore the marriage command. In Genesis 1:28 God blessed Adam and Eve, and commanded them to: 1. *be* fruitful, 2. multiply, and 3. replenish the earth, subdue it and have dominion. This book will only be focusing on the first command.

In the Genesis 1:28 text, God commanded Adam and Eve to be "fruitful" first. He was therefore saying that before you multiply, subdue and dominate, it is important to demonstrate or produce the right fruit in your relationship. When God created mankind (Gen 1:26), He placed the fruit of love in him when He blew His breathe and Adam became a living soul. Adam and Eve's offspring were not only to be the physical fruit of the pair through multiplication, but through the love fruit they would reflect "the image of God".

Love Fruit

The fruit of love was deposited in man when God the Spirit blew the breath of God, and man became a living soul. (Genesis 2:7) They were commanded to be fruit bearers before they were commanded to multiply. After they were told to be fruitful, God then added multiply. God was now saying to them multiply and extend the number of your family, by having loving children and re-people the earth with loving people.

This fruit of love is further described in Gal 5:22-23 as the fruit of the Spirit. This is chaste love. It is pure in thoughts and action! It is modest! Chase love is found in 1 Corinthians 13:4-8. Chase love is pure love…It is a kind of love that chooses to give and act for the betterment of others. **Seek to be a fruit of love mate.**

Jenny and I, along with many other scholars and Christian counsellors believe the fruit Adam and Eve were commanded to be fruitful in was a chaste love, which they demonstrated through the Holy Spirit of God. This kind of love which comes through the indwelling Holy Spirit, does not grow organically and naturally as a physical fruit tree produces good fruit. It requires the constant indwelling presence of Holy Spirit and a willing submission of the indwelt person to activate and live in that chase love.

A natural good fruit is produced without any effort by a good tree; however, the fruit of the Spirit does not come into being automatically. It requires regular partnership between the couple and the Holy Spirit. It demands a heeding of the commands of Scripture and cooperation with the work of the Holy Spirit in the life of the couple.

There are many interpretations and meanings given to the term fruit, but for this book I will only focus upon those that concur with fruit as love:

1. Some have suggested that the singular fruit, stresses the truth that the fruit is one cluster with many individual parts, as one diamond has many facets.
2. Others have suggested that the singular refers to one harvest and the unity of the characteristics that the Spirit produces within the individual.
3. Another possibility is that the fruit of the Spirit is actually one, love, with the other virtues being different manifestations of love in operation. A support of such a view may be 1 Corinthians 13:4-7, where several of the things itemized as fruit in Galatians are included as identifying features of *agape* love.

The fruit of the Holy Spirit that will work in the life of the couples are outlined in Galatians 5:22-23, and can be described as follows: an active love for God and each other; a rejoicing in all kinds of circumstances in marriage; peacefulness and serenity of character and peacemaking among each other; patience and longsuffering with each other; being kind to one another; seeking goodness for each other; remaining faithful and dependable in one's relationship with God and each other; gentle and meek in accepting God's will and in dealing with each other; and the ability to keep oneself in check and under control in all kinds of circumstances for the benefit of the marriage relationship.

Couples entering marriage with the intention to live a lifetime of love and happiness will fail miserably without the enabling Holy Spirit's presence and power. Coming back to the first marriage model and the three commands, God was saying, before you start to multiply, each person must strive to produce mature fruits of love in their lives. Before marriage, it is a good idea to practice serving each other in love. Choose to prefer each other in love. Start living in love before you say, "I Do"! Make sure you are ready to live for the greater good of your partner.

For emphasis, I repeat, the fruit of love was placed in mankind when God the Spirit blew the breath of God in man, and that made him become a living soul. They were commanded to produce loving characteristics before they were commanded to multiply and have children. After they were told to be fruitful, God then added multiplication. God was now saying to them multiply and extend the number of your family by having loving children and re-people the earth with loving people.

Adam and Ever were to pass on the fruit of love to their children as they multiply, subdue and dominate. God commanded Adam and Eve to grow and mature in love for one another, and produce loving children, who would rule their dominion or kingdom in love.

Adam and Eve were commanded to be conduits of love. However, they failed because of sin. Sin caused them to know good and evil! As a result, when they started having their children, one child grew up choosing to love while the other chose to love sin. The loving child was obedient and the other was disobedient. The loving child received the favor of God on his sacrifice and the disobedient child's sacrifice was rejected.

From the beginning, God's intention was a world of loving and worshipping people. Sin short circuited God's purpose, so God sought for another conduit to produce loving people to multiply, subdue and dominate his kingdom. He chose Abram who was later called Abraham. Through Abraham He called Israel as the apple of His eye, but Israel rejected Jesus as the Messiah and today God has called the church to be the model of love to show forth the glory of God in the world. The church should be full of loving people getting married and spreading the love of God to the world.

God has commanded his children to choose to be fruitful. Loving couples! Christians entering marriage should enter with commitment; a lifetime of love. Today, science is telling us that we are wired to love. Yes, we are! However, love is not activated on its own. As couples entering marriage, you must choose to commit and surrender yourselves to the Holy Spirit so that He can help you to give and receive love.

When entering marriage, expect everything in marriage to be done in and through love. To ensure the life of love, God command husbands to lead and model love in the marriage, Ephesians 5:25. Having been married to my wife for over 30 years, I can tell you that it is a mammoth task for husbands. We are not only called to love, but we must also be willing to demonstrate this even to death if necessary; even as Jesus' love led Him to the cross. His love was one of sacrifice. His love for the church is the model for man's love for his wife. But, is it possible to achieve this model? Did God command man to do the impossible? On the contrary! Christ has made it possible for man to love his wife unconditionally through the enabler—the Holy Spirit.

Love's Protocol

Before Paul commanded husbands to love their wives (v. 25), he commanded wives to submit to their own husbands (v. 22), and before Paul commanded the brothers and sisters to submit to each other in the Lord (v. 21), he commanded them to be "filled with the Spirit" (v. 8). God gave men the Holy Spirit to help them achieve the greatest ideal for marriage. Without the aid of the Holy Spirit, it is impossible for husbands to love their wives as Christ outlines in His Word.

While traveling home on a flight from Tortola, British Virgin Islands, I read an interesting article in the *America Way* magazine (February 2, 1999), titled "I Know What Love Is," by Jim Shahin. Jim said that while he was driving his car and listening to Prince's rousing song to immortal love, "I Would Die 4 U," he found out what Prince's idea of love was. "You!"

Prince shouted. "I would die for you."

Singing along with Prince, Jim was not the least bit concerned that the woman in the car next to him was wary of him. As she locked her door and reached for her cell phone, Jim convulsed and banged on the steering wheel of his car as he sang along with Prince. The song questioned, "What if it seemed to her, I was a lunatic?" Then it continued: "I am a lunatic. I am a lunatic of love. I would die for you, darling, if you want me to."

While he sang, Jim suddenly understood the meaning of the song, and he said, "No, you wouldn't, Prince. You wouldn't die for anybody. You're just saying that because it sounds good."

Jim said that in reality Prince would not die for anybody he loved, and few other people would do it either. It was a song with hollow words.

"People say that they will climb mountains, swim oceans, and even die, all to prove their love. But the reality is that they will probably never have to prove it. Wives are not interested in their husbands dying for them. Most wives only ask that their husbands express their love in small ways."

Suppose a husband said to his wife, "Honey, I've decided I'm going to prove my love for you, so I'm leaving today and will be gone for six months to climb Mount Everest. Kiss the kids for me. Don't forget to pay the gas bill. I love you. Bye." What does that kind of love prove? It certainly doesn't prove that this couple has a marriage that God wants for His families.

Love does not focus on self; it is giving, serving, and sharing. By climbing the mountain, the man would be expressing love—not for his wife, but for his sport. He loved the sport of mountain climbing more that he loved her and the children.

Jesus gave Himself for His bride – the church (Ephesians 5:25). He is the supreme model of unconditional love, and it should be noted that Jesus' directive was not for husbands to die for their wives, but to love their wives (5:28). Nevertheless, if the ultimate test of death presents itself, the husbands should be ready to pay the price.

The command, "husbands love your wives" is both simple and complex. The easiest way to show love is in the mundane things. It is giving her a foot massage or making a sandwich and giving her the bigger portion. Show your wife love by telling her that you like her new hairstyle, by picking up after yourself, loading and unloading the dishwasher, and by doing the small things that communicate the message of love and care.

True love is warming up the car in the wintertime before your wife leaves for work. It is going grocery shopping without complaining, then helping her prepare dinner. It is accepting your wife for who she is and at the same time helping her to be all she can be. It is expressing interest in her life—asking about her day. The greatest love can be shown through the little things you do for you wife. Give it some thought! The list is inexhaustible!

As each individual examines the nature of love and the makeup of the person he or she loves, the complexities of love are revealed. According to Hendrix "Real love is an achievement of consciousness and intentionality, a way of being, a hard-won prize granted only to those who persevere" (293).

The command God gave to husbands to love their wives was not an afterthought. Paul gave the example of showing love by using Christ's love for the church as the model (Ephesians 5:23). Paul was motivated to give this command because he wanted to correct the Greek, Roman and Jewish cultural viewpoints on women in general, and wives in particular. A careful reading of the Bible reveals that women were never commanded to love their husbands. Instead, they were encouraged to love their husbands. Paul admonishes the older women to "teach the young women to be sober, to love their husbands, and to love their children" (Titus 2:4, KJV)

Heald states that in Titus 2:4, "The Greek word *philandros* is used to express 'loving your husband.' It is from the root word *Phileo*, which means to show affection, love, devotion, and hospitality. It speaks of being fond of friends and relatives.

The account of the curse placed on women in Genesis 3:16, tell us that God said to the woman [Eve], "I will greatly multiply thy sorrow and the conception; in sorrow thou shalt bring forth children; and thy desire shall be to thy husband" (KJV). It could conclude from the term *thy desire*; that a longing was placed on the woman toward the man in her life. There are, however, various interpretations of this text.

Nevertheless, by the nature of the Curse, a "longing after" was motivated by an intrinsic love for her husband, thus, becoming natural for all other women through the gene of federal mother, Eve. The Hebrew word *teshuwaqah*, interpreted as "desire," means, "sense of stretching out after"—a longing. Therefore, Eve submitted to Adam in love as her natural demeanor before and after the Fall.

The creation story declared that Adam and Eve were created equally in the image of God, and that they were given the rule over everything; they ruled together. The sinful fall in the Garden of Eden brought woman under the rule of the man. However, Christ Jesus died and redeemed man and woman and brought them back into their original state when He became the Second Adam. Once a man and woman accept the finished work of Calvary, they are restored to the perfect image of God. Therefore, husbands should love their wives as copartners and helpmates.

Within our church circle we are inundated with calls in sermons, sermonettes, and comments for wives to be submissive to their husbands; yet, little emphasis is placed upon husbands loving their wives. A careful reading of the Bible, however, reveals that more emphasis is placed on a husband's role to his wife than on the wife's role to her husband. Therefore, as preachers proclaim and teach the gospel, counselor and therapist share, they should carefully prepare, and then present, a balanced approach to sharing of the Word of God. Ministers and counselors must be thorough and comprehensive in this task.

A typical instance is found in Ephesians 5:22-24 when Paul said, "Wives, submit to your own husband as to the Lord. For the husband is the head of the wife, as also Christ is the head of the church; and He is the Savior of the body. Therefore, just as the church is subject to Christ, so let the wives be to their own husbands in everything" (*NKJV*). This directive took only three verses, but reference to the husband's role in marriage took nine verses.

> *Husbands, love your wives, just as Christ also loved the church, and gave Himself for her, that He might sanctify and cleanse her with the washing of water by the word, that He might present her to Himself a glorious church, not having spot, or wrinkle or any such thing; but that she should be holy and without blemish. So, husbands ought to love their own wives as their own bodies; he who loves his wife loves himself. For no one ever hated his own flesh, but nourishes and cherishes it, just as the Lord does the church: For we are members of His body, of His flesh, and of His bones. For this reason, a man shall leave his father and mother, and be joined to his wife, and the two shall be one flesh. This is a great mystery: but I speak concerning Christ and the church. Nevertheless, let each one of you in particular so love his own wife as himself, and let the wife see that she respects her husband (Ephesians 5:25-33, NKJV).*

The crisis in the text is magnified by the extended discourse addressing the problem, the word picture, and the illustration cited.

We are living in a time when it seems that dysfunctional homes, divorced parents, and single-parent families are the norm. Statistics report an alarming growth in single parenting and a decline in two-parent families. In 2013, the United States Census Bureau reported that 62 percent of Americans were single adults; 46 percent of households were headed by single men or women.

Even in our churches today, we find many men separating from their wives and children for various reasons. Abuse is rampant in both single-parent and two-parent families, in Christian and non-Christian families. Many homes do not offer a sense of security to the female members. Sometimes females become prey to their own brothers, fathers or stepfathers, and/or other male members of their families. It is even more alarming that some of these men claim to be Christians.

Let me share with you some simple and practical ideas for you to consider.

Love is not always complex.

It is usually the little things in life that add spice and beauty to love. A major reason for the many dysfunctional homes in the North American families is the lack of love between husbands and wives—specifically the husband's love for his wife. Thanks be to God that men are beginning to reclaim their divinely ordained position in God. An example of this was the Million-Man March in which Louis Farrakkan (one of the Muslim leaders in North America) challenged black men to reclaim their rightful place in their homes, communities, and churches. One problem with this march, however, was that they failed to emphasize that men cannot claim their rightful place in society until they reconcile with Jesus Christ. That has to be achieved first.

There was another "Million-Man March" in Washington D.C., by the Promise Keepers (PK). In this march men of all races, status, and social classes came together, confessed their sins, and pledged to reclaim their rightful places in God's design for men in their families. Even this good intention did not go without criticism. The National Organization for Women (N.O.W.) was outraged claiming that this movement was another white-collar men's movement trying to enslave their wives again and to put them under bondage. Of course, the opposite was true. There have been many reports and testimonies from wives all over North America about the change in their husbands since the march. According to the reports, these men were more loving and compassionate toward their families.

A husband who went to his first Promises Keepers conference in June 1997, at RFK Stadium, in Washington, D.C., said, "That very 'wet' weekend has helped to change my life around. I asked my wife of over 23 years to marry me all over again on Sunday, February 14, 1999, and she did."

Another man by the name of Billy said,

> Eight years ago, I went through a terrible divorce. I made many awful mistakes and I left two kids behind. Since my divorce, I have married a wonderful woman with three kids. Two years ago, all was not well, and the stepfather thing was not working. During that year, I attended the Memphis PK conference. Believe it or not, my boss sort of manipuated me to go.

As soon as I walked into the stadium and heard approximately 50,000 men singing praises to the Lord, I was broken. The main thing I remember is that I cried for the entire weekend. I cried over leaving my two kids in my first marriage, I cried over the tough time I was having with my step kids, and I cried because I knew I was not much of a husband, a father, or a man . . . what a mess!

When I got home from Memphis, I was determined to be a dad to all of my kids. I wanted to be responsible. The two years since my first PK conference have been awesome. All of my children, all five of them, are doing well. I have a relationship with each one of them. God has given me a family, and I love them very much. I have really made an effort to be responsible to those I love. It feels so good to do the right thing.

This year, in Little Rock, my 16-year-old stepson and I attended a PK conference together. It was so great to stand and praise God together! My relationship with my stepson is nothing short of a God-given miracle. I still have a lot to learn, but I just wanted to say thanks for showing me how to leave a legacy. Trust me, I thank God daily for what I have now.

Most men went home from that Promise Keepers meeting with their consciences raised and with a deeper commitment to family values. However, even if the experience received by the men at the Promise Keepers meeting was short lived, it was worth the changes that took place in homes. I have read the confessions and the testimonies of many of the men who attended these meetings and can say with a certainty that Promise Keepers does not need to apologize for the positive outcomes.

Another men's group that was recently formed is called The Men of the Titanic. The group was organized to honor the bravery and valor of men who have given their lives in watery graves for their wives. Some women who wanted to keep the memory of these men alive started The Men of the Titanic. Their theme was *We Won't Forget*. The ladies eventually faded out, but later a group of men resurrected the movement to honor the memories, lives and love stories of the men of the Titanic. They pledged to adopt the same philosophy that the original organization had in their relationship with their wives. The simple philosophy of this movement is that each man pledges to love his wife to the point of death. These men declared that if a decision were made to take their wives' lives, they would volunteer their lives instead so their wives would be saved, just as many of the men did in the real *Titanic* crisis. It is encouraging that this men's group is motivated by such high morals and standards, and its motivation was reignited with the debut of the movie *Titanic*. We men are no longer our own, but sons of God through the reconciliation of Jesus Christ, are motivated to love our wives whom God has given to us, even to the point of death if the ultimate test should come.

Lead by Love

When the command for husbands to love their wives was given, it did not mean to subjugate, exert power, manipulate, coerce, intimidate or abuse. The command simply **means that husbands should lead, serve and care for their wives by loving actions.** It begins first with husbands choosing to obey the command of God in Genesis 1:28 and Ephesians 5:25 to Biblically love their wives.

Men need to make that intentional choice before they become husbands. Husbands are commanded to love their wives with God's love. That is, God's unconditional love. Love is neither a seasonable nor a one-time event. It is an ongoing, unconditional exercise. Whatever husbands need to do to show love, God is holding them responsible for their families by how well they love their wives.

It is disturbing, but some fathers show more love to their children than they do to their wives. You may grow in a home where this kind of love was shown. Men are to love their children, but the love for their wives should not conflict with that love. Giving romance, money, and gifts does not fulfill God's call for husbands to love their wives. These things are superficial even though to some women they are signs of love. Even if you give your wife all the tangible items she desires, she still may be missing genuine love. Many husbands and fathers are good men, good fathers, and good supporters but poor lovers. And many husbands only give love to their wives at special times. The command to love your wife is not seasonal; it is a command for all times.

Love is the only thing a husband can give his wife to make her completely happy and satisfied. All other things are secondary and not fully satisfying, but when they get love, they have it all. Love is the ultimate, love is infinite, and, most of all, love is priceless.

It is amazing to look at some couples. As they grow older, they become more close-knit in their love relationship. On the other hand, there are some couples who drift apart the longer they live together. When you get married, your love should create a bond that, with time, is unbreakable. When you get married and you find that your wife or your husband is not as attractive, appealing, or appetizing as time passes, then you need to check your "love thermometer" to see what has changed. It is important to not just look at the physical beauty as inner beauty, character and grace are just as important.

Brother, the wife you are about to marry is beautiful; she is as precious jewels. Your love and attention will keep her shining, glowing, glittering and blooming. God has designed women to function best in an environment of love. If true love is given, your wife will be able to function effectively and make her contribution to the loving home that God intends for you to rear your children in. Sister, the man you are about to marry deserves your love and respect every day that you are his wife. A man who knows he is loved and respected will give you the world.

Amidst the crisis in the first family, Adam and Eve stayed together in love and weathered the storms of separation from the Garden of Eden and the murder of their son Cain by his brother Abel. Love is not easy. Love can cause pain, bitterness, resentment, and disappointment; but, if you keep giving love, it will hide a multitude of faults, sins, errors or flaws, and will ultimately replace all negatives with positives. If it is love that brings two lives and hearts together as one, and if God is an essential part of that equation, then whatever circumstances may come one's way, a married couple can salvage their love relationship just as the first family, Adam and Eve, did.

The Garden of Eden suffered a great physical loss when sin entered. Adam and Eve were cast out of the garden to live in a place that was not as pleasant as Eden had been, but they kept the garden within their hearts as they shared love and enjoyed life to the fullest. They lived together weathering various family problems, and they died at an old age still loving each other (5:5).

As you look forward to the reality of marriage, remember, problems will always be a part of marriage. However, when chaste love is present before marriage, (the kind of love where one abstains from sexual intercourse before marriage) all the internal and external forces that might want to destroy your relationship will crumble and healing and resolution will flow to keep your relationship whole. If you demonstrate chaste love, regardless of the circumstances you will face in your relationship, the Holy Spirit will help build a relationship and a life that will show forth the glory of God in your marriage when you say, "I do.

Discussion

1. Do you believe it is possible to achieve the model of God's love for your marriage?
2. What are some ways you can express your love to your spouse?
3. What type of love did Adam have that kept him and Eve together even in tough, life-changing experiences?
4. Is this love available today?
5. What is the Holy Spirit's role in making Chaste lover?

Chapter 2

The Modes of Love

"I love you", is one of the most used terms in the world. Yet, the word, "love" has the potential to be one of the most misunderstood words in the English language. It is very difficult to interpret its meaning when it is used by itself. In the English language, the meaning is only understood in the context of how it is spoken or written. These words can create difficulty in the marriage relationship if the phrase is not used properly. It has the potential to create serious communication problems. Communication is listed as one of the main reasons for marital problems and divorce. It is also a major problem if we cannot express our thoughts using the correct words. Couples entering marriage need to know how to express love as the Genesis narrative commanded in order to be fruitful (Genesis 1:26) - which will be discussed later in the book.

Being fruitful in love will include loving with the right knowledge, service, and commitment. To help us better understand love we need to look at the Greek language which provides us a wide range of words that best describes love. In the Greek language, there are five words that are used to describe love, (1) *agape*, unconditional love; (2) *eros*, romantic love; (3) *Phileo*, friendship; (4) *Storge*, belonging; and (5) *epithumia*, lovemaking.

These words will be my focus in this chapter as I discuss how couples entering marriage can choose the right word, at the right time, to express the right meaning, and get the right result.

The English-language definition of love is limited in scope and range. Therefore, as couple, you must understand the command to love by using the Greek etymology of love; not the Greek mythology of love!

The Greek meaning of the word *love* used in Ephesians 5:25, Agape, refers to the kind of love that God wants husbands to exhibit towards their wives.

Agape Love – Loving unconditionally

Agape love is a selfless and unselfish love; a giving and sacrificial love. It is the love of the mind and will, as well as, of the heart. It is not only a love of affection and feelings; it is a love of will and commitment. It is the love that works for the highest good even if the person does not deserve to be loved.

Jesus' love for the church is the pattern God set for husbands' love toward their wives. When this type of love is given, wives will melt in their husbands' arms and willingly accept their loving authority as leader of the family.

In a Christian marriage, *agape* is the foundation upon which all other love must be built. If a husband does not base his love for his wife on *agape* love, it will not stand the trials and tests of time. In "unconditional love" God is saying to the husband that as Christ loves the church so should he love his wife—unconditionally. Unconditional love is an action that you make happen. It is a love you determine to give without performance. You love whether or not the other desires your love. It requires knowledge; finding out what makes your partner needs to feel loved. It expects nothing in return; it is a gift.

It is very important that couples entering marriage make this mental decision of loving unconditionally, before they say, "I do." Counselors, ministers and therapists know that the strongest love that will be leading you to the altar might not be Agape love. It might be one of the other four, like Eros ... romance or Storge ... sense of belonging. What will keep the marriage viable and strong is first and foremost unconditional love. The others might change depending on situations, but unconditional love is unconditional. It loves whether or not!

Brother, as you prepare for marriage, understand your position to love. Paul did not leave the command for husbands to love their wives to their own interpretations; instead, he elaborated by saying that the husband is to have the same love for his wife that he has for his own body (Ephesians 5:28). This means that the husband is to nourish and cherish his wife. The word *nourish* (*ektrephei*) means to feed, clothe, nurture, and look after her until she is mature in the marriage and then to continue nourishing her as long as she lives. The word *cherish* (*thalpei*) means to hold within the heart; to treat with warmth, tenderness, care, affection, and appreciation.

What a difference would exist in your marriage when you choose to nourish and cherish your wife as you do to your own bodies! Think about the meanings of *nourished* and *cherished* for just a moment, then imagine the quality of life that would take place in your marriage.

It is important to note that the New Testament provides a great treatise on love. Paul's understanding and discussion of love makes it a central theme in his writing. His use of the noun *agape* makes that term almost a technical one. Prior to

Paul, the Greek term *agape* was seldom used. Paul took this seldom used term and filled it with Christian meaning. This love about which Paul wrote is somewhat different from the love we normally experience and speak about.

Christian love is not simply an emotion which arises because of the character of the one loved, nor is it due to the loving quality of the lover. The love of a child of God is *agape* love—unconditional love. It is a relationship of self-giving which results from God's activity in Christ. The source of Christian love is God (Romans 5:8), and the believer's response of faith makes love a human possibility (5:5). *Agape* lays the foundation for *eros* to flourish.

Marcia smiled at the text that Roger sent her. She looked forward to his texts every day when he went to lunch. Sometimes that was what got her through the day whenever she was having a bad day at work. Even the long drive home felt shorter whenever she remembered his daily texts.

Do you think this is good practice for Roger and should he keep this up even when they are married?

Eros Love – Romantic

Eros is seen in our culture as sex. However, in the Greek usage, *eros* refers to romantic love which gives you the thrills and sweeps you off your feet. This love takes effort to grow! This type of love has saturated our culture to the extent that the Christian community has avoided it like a plague! Romance is a natural biological response. It is how it is governed and dealt with that determines its sanctity. The Bible is not silent on romance. Let him kiss me with the kisses of his mouth-- for your love is more delightful than wine. (Solomon's Song of Songs 1:1-2 NIV) {2} Oh how warm the Shulamite must have felt when she heard Solomon's romantic words. Just like Marcia reading the text from Roger.

These verses from the Song of Songs flow from a romantic man who reflects the heart of a passionate God. Theologians call the story of redemption a "divine romance" and that is certainly appropriate. In the images of marriage reflected in Scripture, betrothal and romance are among the best known and deepest parallels to the love of God for His people. God is love and God is romantic.

Scripture speaks of a God who is passionately in love with His Creation. In (Hosea 11:8-9 NIV) God said, "How can I give you up, Ephraim? How can I hand you over, Israel? How can I treat you like Admah? How can I make you like Zeboiim? My heart is changed within me; all my compassion is aroused. {9} I will not carry out my fierce anger, nor will I turn and devastate Ephraim. For I am God, and not man-- the Holy One among you. I will not come in wrath. God is involved, He loves, He grieves, He feels.

God made human beings as romantic being! And, true romance is always heterosexual!

The biblical model of romance is between Christ and the Church and between a bridegroom and His bride. The romance that is written about in the Song of Songs is unashamedly heterosexual. It celebrates the differences between the genders. As a point of information, the Hebrew/Christian's view of romance is never asexual or homosexual.

The Beloved

In every romance there is "the beloved". Our beloved is God and God's beloved is His Church. In marriage the wife is the beloved of the husband and vice-versa. The "beloved" is special. This attraction begins before marriage and continues in marriage. Your beloved is beautiful, chosen and different from any other person. Once your beloved is chosen there is an elevation in status that defies reason, fairness or justice and which is pure grace.

Solomon says, "My beloved is mine and I am his; he pastures his flock among the lilies." My beloved is mine and I am his." (Song of Songs 2:16 NRSV) that is part of romance. Christian romance is not "unguarded". Christian romance cherishes the beloved to the exclusion of all competition. Romance allows the beloved to "possess" you. As the love expressed in the Song of Songs matures there is a slight but significant reversal of 2:16 in 6:3. I am my beloved's and my beloved is mine; he pastures his flock among the lilies. (Song of Songs 6:3 NRSV) Do you notice the difference? Now she says "I am my beloved's" first of all. Instead of her joy being first of all in having him as her lover she now rejoices first of all in being his. She has matured. She has surrendered to love. The secret to Christian romance is that it honors the lover and the beloved.

Honor

The Scripture and not culture is what governs our romance. "Husbands, in the same way, show consideration for your wives in your life together, paying honor to the woman as the weaker sex, since they too are also heirs of the gracious gift of life--so that nothing may hinder your prayers." (1 Peter 3:7 NRSV) His legs are pillars of marble set on bases of pure gold. His appearance is like Lebanon, choice as its cedars. {16} His mouth is sweetness itself; he is altogether lovely. This is my lover, this is my friend, O daughters of Jerusalem (Song of Songs 5:15-16 NIV). Romantic expressions should be shown with respect and honor for the beloved. Romance honors the other. It is OK to put your beloved up on a pedestal. Yes, I am advocating a romantic love that finds the good and which pays attention to it.

"I don't see what all the fuss is about romance." George and Karen were at a conference for couples who were considering marriage. Karen was concerned because this was not the first time George had made that statement since they started dating.

She laughed at the statement but deep down she was worried that he was serious.

Is all the fuss about romance necessary or not?

In romantic love the kind of honor given to the one you love can seem extreme and exaggerated. Even a cursory reading of the Song of Songs dumbfounds a lot people. It is hard to conceive the level of romantic love that is expressed. Is this a ghost relationship or a real one between Solomon and his wife? The truth is, most readers will never fully understand the poetical expressions, except in the eyes of the beloved.

Here are three action tips to fulfill *eros* love:

1. Think about your partner throughout the day.
2. Think about the romantic moments you have spent with each other.
3. Plan for romance without limit to your imagination—be creative.

Let's take a look at some additional Greek words for love and their meanings.

Earl lost count of the times he looked at the clock on the restaurant wall since 7 pm. Charlene was still at work at minutes to 10 for the 3rd day this week. This had become a pattern and no matter how many times he spoke about it, she always said the same thing.

"Do you think I can make it to the head of the company by doing what everyone else is doing"?

Earl had lost count of the amount of times that Charlene had stood him up since they started dating. He wanted to spend more time with her just hanging out but she always seemed so busy.

As he left the restaurant he wondered if he was doing the right thing by asking her to marry him. Is Earl justified in having these misgivings or will Charlene change once they are married?

How can they resolve this?

Phileo Love - Friendship

Phileo is that friendship which produces closeness and companionship. It is to be a friend, to be fond of (an individual), i.e., having affection for; denoting personal attachment. It is here that time is spent just sharing intimate thoughts; reminiscing on whatever comes to mind. It is in this time of sharing of your thoughts and emotions that you build closeness, oneness and a soul bond with your partner.

There are many married couples that are living like single people. Their lives are so busy they have no time for each other. True friends make time for each other, and your spouse should be your best friend.

Invest quality time with your beloved now. Earl was longing for more time with Charlene to build Phileo love. It is in these times that you build loving memories that will help you in the days ahead when you say I do. Take the time to build friendship with your spouse. Grow not only as romantic lovers but also as friends. The Bible tells us a friend sticketh closer than a brother. (Proverbs 18:24) Many couples wander away from being friends to being wife, husband, mother, father, or caregiver. They then turn to find friends outside the marriage which can lead to marital challenges. Spend time doing things together before you say, I do, then, after you say I do, continue to do things together and build the bond of friendship.

Storge Love - Familial Love

Storge is that feeling of belonging and security. Having a sense of belonging in marriage means that partner feels accepted. A sense of belonging is a human need, just like the need for food and shelter. Hence, feeling that you belong is an important part of the marital dynamics. It places value in the relationship and help you cope with the challenges that life will bring in the marriage.

Many people today, who are entering marriage, go in with a lone ranger mentality. They believe they do not need anyone or any support systems. Some see themselves as connected only to one or two people. Couples who choose to enter marriage with the storge love will find that community improves marital motivation, health, and happiness. When you are connected to others, you will realize that all people struggle and have difficult times. You will see the testimonies of others and the faithfulness of God. You will realize that you are not alone, and this gives you comfort and hope.

> *So, as you prepare for marriage here are three communal belongings and blessings you should seek and get before you say, "I do."*

Secure the favor of God, parental approval, friends support and the blessings of church leaders and church community. When these ingredients are missing in the marriage foundation it can create unnecessary, unbearable hardships for couples and families. Many lives have been destroyed because of the absence of these communal blessings. It has created irreparable emotional wounds for innocent children who stand helplessly by as their parents tolerate or terminate painful relationships and contract new ones.

Epithumia Love – Sex Lovemaking

Epithumia is "sex lovemaking," an art that develops with time. One of the problems with *epithumia* love is that many individuals enter into a marriage relationship with the wrong concept of lovemaking. The view of many people about lovemaking is determined by their premarital experiences or by the false slow-motion, choreographed movie scenes.

As a result of faulty expectations, many husbands and wives struggle in the art of lovemaking. Also, because of the over saturated sexual culture of the 21st century many are truly illiterate about the value of sex. To truly appreciate the value of epithumia in marriage Christians should do all they can to avoid having sex before marriage.

A growing body of research finds that premarital sex undermines the chances for a successful marriage. According to Sheridan, studies performed at Cornell University (600 married couples), Brigham Young University (2,035 married couples) and Macquarie University in Australia have all subscribed to the same conclusions:

- Sex before marriage can adversely impact the romance and sex lives of couples after they marry.
- The earlier couples began having sex in their relationship, the more it's likely to limit their future growth as a couple. This is especially true if sexual relations begin in the first several months of the relationship. The longer couples wait the better; waiting until the wedding night appears to result in the strongest marriages.
- The more sexual partners a person has before marriage, the lower the chances for enjoying romantic feelings after marriage.

Sheridan went on to say that the group included in the Brigham Young University study was above average regarding premarital sex:

- 84 percent had sex before marriage; a majority had sex within two months of when they started dating;
- 16 percent delayed intercourse until marriage.

Dean Busby, who led the study, reported:

- couples who waited to have sex until marriage described the quality of their marital sex life higher (15 percent),
- the stability of their marriage stronger (22 percent higher)
- their overall relationship satisfaction higher (20 percent) than those who did not wait.

The Cornell study explains why: "A strong sexual desire may thwart the development of other key ingredients of a healthy relationship, such as commitment, mutual understanding or shared values "(Sheridan).

Other studies involving the sex hormones oxytocin, dopamine and vasopressin provide more explanation on the effect of sex before marriage. They say, these hormones are released in heavy amounts during sexual relations. When these hormones are released, they create a good feeling; they also create a feeling of emotional connection with our sexual partner.

The report further says that if the premarital sex is with the same partner, the bonding effect is powerful. However, if the sex partner changes, the hormone-induced bonding weakens, as if it's diluted. What is the impact of premarital sex you asked? It sadly affects the marriage relationship.

If Christians want to have healthy marriages in their future, they need to adhere to the biblical prohibitions, read the studies on the impact of sex before marriage and understand the science revelation. If you are dating or courting you will do better to cease all sexual practices and focus your time on learning about each other — their beliefs, their likes and dislikes, their families, their hopes and dreams for the future, how to trust and rely on each other — and develop a committed relationship. Delaying sexual relations helps strengthen marriages and improve marital sex lives.

It is important to note that the Bible is silent on physical techniques, but it addresses the marriage rights (Exodus 21:10), erotic caresses (Song of Solomon 2:6; 7:1-9), fondling (Genesis 26:8), and pleasure in conceiving (Genesis 18:12). Yet, these are set forth in the context of the behavior of married couples.

Intimate sexual behavior outside of marriage is considered sexual immorality from the Biblical perspective. Since the Bible is silent on the intimate details of lovemaking, each spouse should govern the decisions in the bedroom. The Song of Solomon celebrates God's gift of bodily love between man and woman as it is portrayed in Genesis 2:23-25. In that passage, the Creator's wisdom and bounty are displayed. So, couples do not be bashful! Our Creator designed lovemaking for pleasure and procreation.

Here are four simple suggestions to enjoy *epithumia* when you are married. God created us as sexual beings and we all have needs for fulfillment.
1. It is appropriate to think "sexy" about your spouse.
2. Focus on the joy and pleasure of lovemaking. However, there will be times when your desire for lovemaking will not be mutual.
3. Discuss this issue with your spouse and come to a compromise; thus, both will be fulfilled.
4. Discuss the likes and dislikes of lovemaking with your spouse. Read books on techniques and be utterly creative! Become a 24-hour lover. It takes time to set the pace and create the environment so each partner can savor the ambiance.

Love is one of the most powerful and greatest gifts of life. It is a wonderful gift, which when released produces an ecstatic experience. In the Old Testament we find Solomon, in his Biblical wisdom, talking about love: "Love is as strong as death . . . Many waters cannot quench love . . . If one were to give all the wealth of his house for love, it would be utterly scorned" (8:6, 7, *NIV*). Solomon also indicates that there is a right time and place for love when he said, "Daughters of Jerusalem, I charge you. . . . Do not arouse or awaken love until it so desires" (3:5, *NIV*). In these poems love is portrayed in its power, splendor, and freshness, and in devotion to each other. Love takes many forms—moments of union and separation, ecstasy and anguish, longing and fulfillment.

The Love Sage Wisdom

Study the Book of Song of Solomon. Any couple in love needs to look carefully at Song of Solomon to obtain lessons on how to love each other. The following love themes will reveal so much to you about love that it will add spice to your love life:

> Longing is a part of love (1:1-8).
> Love will not be silent (1:9-2:7).
> Spring and love go together (2:8-17).
> Love is exclusive (3:1-5).
> Love is enhanced by friendship (3:6-11).
> Love sees only the beautiful (4:1-7).
> Love involves giving and receiving (4:8-5:1).
> Love means risking the possibility of pain (5:2-6:3).
> Words fail for expressing love (6:4-7:9).
> Love must be given freely (7:10-13).
> True love is priceless (8:1-14).

God is the source of love and He places that love in the human heart. The believer must then actualize that love. God is love, and the man or woman who receives God receives love. God commanded husbands to love their wives. He gave birth to that unconditional love when He redeemed man.

Paul's command to Christians to love the nature of love as self-giving is clear in Galatians 5:13-15. The Christian walk is to be characterized by love, so Paul speaks of "walking in love" (Romans 14:15). The Christian is to increase and abound in love (1 Thessalonians 3:12).

Love is vitally connected with faith; in that the believer's faithful response is one of love. Love is also connected with hope. Christian love is evidence of God's purpose for His children. The Johannine writings magnify the significance of love as forcefully and fully as any other writings. John's writings account for only one-tenth of the New Testament, but they provide one-third of the references to love. The key passage is Jesus' new commandment in John 13:34, 35: "I

The Modes of Love

give you a new commandment, that you love one another. Just as I have loved you, you also should love one another. By this everyone will know that you are my disciples, if you have love for one another."

Jesus' command that we love one another gives us insight into the nature of His desire for the church—the nature of Christian love. What is commanded is not an emotion. It is the disciplined will to seek the welfare of others. Jesus speaks with the authority of the Father, the only One with authority to make such demands of men and women. Jesus speaks as the incarnate Word (John 1:1, 14). He has authority to give conditions for discipleship. Notice the relationship of this commandment to that found in Leviticus 19:18. Both passages command love, but Jesus' commandment includes the clause "as I have loved you."

The letters of John make explicit statements about the ethical implications of love. Our appreciation of these letters and the command to love is increased when we realize that John's opponents claimed that they loved God despite their unlovely temper and conduct. They claimed enlightenment and communion with God. (They were Gnostics or "Knowers.") The Old Testament, which was John's basis for Christians, portrays belief in Jesus and love for one another (1 John 3:23). This love is to be manifested in deeds (v. 18). John left no doubt about the relationship of love and belief in God. Whoever hates his brother is in the darkness (2:9). Whoever does not do right and love his brother is not of God (4:20). First John 4:8 is the climax: "He that loveth not knoweth not God; for God is love."

The simple theme of 1 Corinthians 13 reveals the power of love. An outline of that chapter declares the importance of love, (vv. 1-3); the acts of love (vv. 4-7); the permanence of love (vv. 8-12); and the supremacy of love (v. 13).

All through the Old and New Testaments we see how important love is for the community of faith and marriage. Therefore, if love is one of the main hallmarks of Christianity, how much more then should this love be practiced by redeemed husbands and wives.

Many of our Christian brothers have entered into their relationship with a faulty Scriptural interpretation on submission, headship, the glory of the woman and silence in the church; as a result, their relationship is not full of love as the heavenly Father designed marriage to be. Faulty interpretation of Scripture causes many marriages to go sour, and ultimately, they end with abuse. But there is hope! Journey with as we explore these issues together.

It is a difficult task to truly love your spouse if we do not fully know or understand each other as the Scriptures declares. To know in this sense refers to an acquired knowledge of the male/female specie according to the design of the Creator. One of the major reasons many couples are failing in their love relationship with their spouses is based on faulty experiences (culture and tradition), lack of understanding of men/women role as outlined in Scripture, and lack of knowledge about how to express their love. It appears that some men find it difficult to fully understand women emotionally. I am not sure if we men can! But brothers and sisters can know each other from a biblical point of view and ultimately to appreciate and love each other as the Word commands.

The "Gift" to Love

God designed and created the perfect gift for man—woman. He made this woman by using the rib of Adam as His raw material and she was created to complement, and complete God's plan for life. She was presented to Adam as a perfect and permanent gift; one who would be a lifetime partner, to love and to cherish, and one who would supply all his needs for companionship, pleasure and procreation. She was designed as a suitable partner. No other created being could replace her, and neither was there any other created being that could take her place in the life of Adam. She was the perfect match.

When God presented Adam with this "*gift*," his wife, Adam confessed that she was indeed a suitable and compatible partner for him when he said, "bone of my bones and flesh of my flesh" (v. 23).

Before Adam received this gift, he was living a life that was not complete; he was lonely. He had no one to share his thoughts or his dreams; he had no one to work alongside him. However, when he received Eve, his life was finally complete, and his world was changed.

As Christians prepare to enter marriage, I believe that all brothers should see their wives as "*gifts*" given by God to be loved and cherished. There are many brothers who see their wives as gifts on the day they are married, but after the wedding and the honeymoon, they no longer see them as gifts from God, but as possessions they own and control. Wives are not the properties of men. Instead, they are gifts from God to men and as such, husbands must honor God's gift by loving their wives as Christ loves the church.

Grace screamed in frustration as the bus drove off from the curb. She would have to wait another hour for the next bus and that would mean getting home late. She knew that Ken would make a fuss if she got home too late.

He called her house phone like clockwork every evening at 7pm and lately he has been getting on her nerves with the constant arguments over this.

They were not even married yet and already she felt trapped. Ken believed that a woman should not work outside the home and he was trying to find every reason to justify this belief. According to him how would she be able to get home on time when they got married to prepare his meal?

Is there cause for alarm here?

Scripture teaches that a marriage based and founded on love is a complete, fulfilled and successful marriage. Husbands are called in Scripture to be the head of their families. Scripture calls husbands to lead their families, by loving their wives—their gifts from God. In order to love your wife in the manner required, brothers you must not only understand the original design of wives as gifts, but the evolutionary process women have gone through. Methods and ways of demonstrating love have changed every decade. It is the responsibility of each brother to discover ways of showing love to his wife and keeping that love alive.

A 1997report revealed that only 15 percent of wives worked outside the home in 1955. By 1990, that percentage had increased to 55 percent. These changes in the role of women have influenced how brothers show love to their wives. Because many husbands today are no longer the sole financial provider of the household, they must learn to adjust to that dynamic. Brothers need to remember when they come home from work; their wives will also be coming home from work. They will both be tired. Therefore, both must learn to communicate and agree on ways and when to demonstrate love toward each other.

The role of Church and Jesus as a Love Model

In order for husbands to truly love their wives they need to understand the love relationship between Jesus and the church and the standard He set—how men and women were made and how women were treated in Bible times.

Christ loves the church by choice—voluntarily and freely—and has made it the object of His love. The church was by nature sinful. We know that the church of Christ is made up of people who are actually defiled by their own transgressions; but the kind of love that Jesus bestows on the church is that of a husband. His love is special, constant, true and intense. It is saturated with appreciation for the original design, evolutionary process, and potential for the church. It is not mere lip service. By nature, the church is not yet perfected for Christ, but by grace He entitled her to His love and forgiveness. It is important to note that neither wives nor husbands are perfect. However, it is the husband's responsibility to give love to his wife, as a gift of grace, so that together they will become whole in the marriage union.

In the Garden, Adam and Eve were created equal and complemented each other (Genesis 1:27, 28; 2:18-23). The New Testament teaches that in Christ this Edenic completeness is restored (2 Corinthians 5:17; Galatians 3:28; Ephesians 5:21-33). Mates are equal (1 Corinthians 7:4) and interdependent (1 Corinthians 11:11, 12); the new creation in Christ makes this possible.

The fall ruptured God's plan for male/female equality and produced sin. Sin produced male dominance and female submissiveness (Genesis 3:16). Hence, many scholars believe that male dominance and female submissiveness are "descriptive rather than prescriptive." Careful investigation of the Old Testament, specifically the Book of Genesis, reveals that much of Scripture describes a double standard for male superiority and female inferiority; a kind of "chain of command" where the husband is found ruling his wife and children. Different standards of fidelity in marriage are also quite apparent in Old Testament scripture.

Unfaithful wives were dealt with more severely than husbands were (Numbers 5:11-31; Deuteronomy 22:22-29). However, the New Testament response was that of mutual equality and servanthood toward each other with the servanthood of Jesus as the basic criterion (Ephesians 5:21-33).

In the eyes of Christ, husbands and wives are equal. However, in light of functions, the Bible teaches an order for marriage. The order is very simple; the husband, as the head, should be giving loving care to his wife; and the wife should voluntarily submit to the loving care of her husband. When this method is adhered to, even the children will follow suite in the family hierarchical structure as outlined in Ephesians 6:1-3.

> *Children obey your parents in the Lord, for this is right. Honor your father and mother—which is the first commandment with a promise—that it may go well with you and that you may enjoy long life on the earth (NIV).*

Sisters are not only given as gifts to their husbands, but they are given as gifts to work alongside their husbands as they serve their families, church, communities, nations, and the world. Throughout the New Testament we find examples of husband and wife teams actively involved in ministry.

Discussion

1. How do you build your friendships?
2. Do you do things (recreational/social) together?
3. Do you share moments together?
4. What are your thoughts on the types of love mentions?
5. How will they relate to your marriage?
6. Do you find it difficult to give or accept unconditional love?
7. Do you nourish and cherish your lover?
8. If you nourished and cherished your spouse, would there be a change in your relationship.
9. What is the difference between a Scripture-based marriage and one that is not Scripture-based?
10. List and discuss some of the husband and wife teams in the New Testament.

Chapter 3

Complimentary Love

Mark looked at Navelette and shook his head. She was at it again! From the day they started dating all she did was find fault. She had never complimented him on anything. He was beginning to wonder if he should stop preaching because Navelette always found something in his sermons to pick at. Even though many persons would tell him what a good job he did; everything went out the window because the woman he loved and was going to marry seemed to find it so easy to tear him down.

Is this mind over matter?

One of the hardest things in life for some people is how to receive compliments graciously. There are a few peoples who also find it difficult to give compliments. Compliment is very necessary and an essential part of life, but more so, in love and marriage.

People have a tendency to see the negative side of things and to focus on the negatives rather than the positives. Focusing on the negatives hides or obscures the positive attributes. Wherever there is a negative there is always a positive. Choose to see the positive and it will provide you with more than you can find to be complimentary about. Married life is filled with both positive and negative realities. There will be things you like and some you don't. Choose to look for the positive and build on the positive by being a complimentary lover.

"I don't care what the board says, no woman will be on the officer's board in my church." Marva looked at her husband to be and wondered if she was doing the right thing when she accepted his proposal.

She believed that women were just as capable as men in leadership positions in the church but Lennox was so against this.

Would this become a source of contention later?

There are many people in our culture, and sad to say, even in the church that underestimate the worth of women because the Scripture speaks more about men. It is important to note that the Bible was written by men, inspired of the Holy Spirit, to articulate the plan of God for His people; not to elevate one sex above the other. Both male and female play an active part in the evolutionary process of salvation.

The picture of woman revealed in the Bible is far from one-dimensional. Frequently subjected to the rule of her male counterpart, often adored for her beauty and purity, and occasionally praised for her leadership in times of crisis, woman emerges from the pages of the Bible with as much complexity as man. Women in Bible times lived in a patriarchal society.

Both the Old and New Testament worlds normally restricted the role of women primarily to the sphere of home and family, although a few strong women emerged as leaders. In religious life woman was subordinate to man. Her father and then her husband, or other male relatives, gave her protection and direction.

Jesus opened the boundaries for women. He paid attention to them. His manner was inclusive as He acknowledged their place in the Kingdom. He elevated the status of women (the other rib) by what He did and what He said. In addition, He affirmed the worth and value of women. Paul also caught Jesus' vision. Although Paul faced the need to preserve order in the early church, he exclaimed in Galatians 3:28: "There is neither Jew nor Greek, there is neither bond nor free, there is neither male nor female: for ye are all one in Christ Jesus." The final barrier preventing women from fully participating in the kingdom of God, toppled under Jesus' influence.

The Old Testament shows women in at least two views. The predominant view is one of woman in subjection to man. However, at times, a woman is also the object of adoration and admiration. The creation narratives in Genesis foreshadow two different perspectives regarding women. In Genesis 1:27, man and woman are created simultaneously in the thoughts of God. Woman, like man, is made in the image of God. Together, man and woman reflect the image of God. A woman was not in an inferior place in creation nor was she an afterthought of God. A godly woman is made as a companion, a suitable helper to compliment her husband.

Genesis 2:7-25 tells us that man was created before woman, but in this account, woman was viewed as being created for man as his helper. This account is often cited as supportive of the view that woman should remain subjected to man since she has a subordinate position in creation; but the narrative describes woman as a "suitable partner" (v. 20, *REB*) for whom man leaves his father and mother.

The subordination of woman appears more clearly in a close reading of the Ten Commandments. The Commandments are addressed to men, a fact evidenced by the use of masculine pronouns. A major evidence of women's subordination is the reference to man not to covet any of his neighbor's property. His wife is included in the list of possessions (Exodus 20:17).

Marriage and divorce were areas in which a woman's rights were subordinate to those of a man's. If a woman, who was about to be married, was suspected of not being a virgin, she was required to submit to a test. If the test proved she was not a virgin, she could be stoned to death at her father's door (Deuteronomy 22:13-21). This requirement was not necessary for the man. If a man and woman were caught in the act of adultery, both of them were stoned. Adultery was a crime against the husband's rights, and the stoning vindicated those rights (Deuteronomy 22:22).

A husband who was jealous of his wife, and had some fears about her faithfulness, could take her to the priest and have her submit to an intricate test to determine her innocence or guilt (Numbers 5:11-31). However, if a wife suspected her husband of being unfaithful, she did not have the same right to confront her husband.

Divorce was always slanted toward the husband. He could obtain a divorce from his wife "because he finds something objectionable about her" (Deuteronomy 24:1). The Jews variously interpreted the phrase "something objectionable," and it ran the gamut from adultery to burned toast!

Inequity between boy and girl babies existed from the very beginning of life. A mother who bore a girl baby was considered unclean twice as long as a mother who bore a male baby. During her time of purification, after the birth of her baby, a mother was not to "touch any holy thing, or come into the sanctuary, until the days of her purification are completed" (Leviticus 12:4b).

Proverbs 31 gives a picture of the hardworking, praiseworthy, "virtuous" woman. Yet, woman's most positive image was that of wife and mother. Against the predominant pattern of woman in subordinate roles, several positive images emerged from the Old Testament. The birth of children was a sign of God's favor bestowed upon a woman. A particular sign of God's favor was the birth of male children (Genesis 29:31-30:24). Her position as wife and mother undoubtedly venerated her.

The Ten Commandments cite a son's duty to honor both his father and mother (Exodus 20:12). The ideal woman, eulogized in Proverbs 31, was a wife and mother who industriously fulfilled both roles, in addition to engaging profitably in the business world.

The story of Ruth is a good example of a traditional woman admired for her role as a good daughter-in-law. Ruth and Naomi, whose husbands died, were women of worth whom God aided by sending Boaz as their protector (1-4). A thread that crosses the dominant pattern of the subjection of woman is one that depicts her positively. Wisdom, which held high value for the Hebrew people, was personified as "she" (Proverbs 1:20; 7:4). The prophet Isaiah used a mother's love for her child as a model for God's love for His people (Isaiah 49:15; 66:13). Several women—Miriam, Deborah, Huldah, and Esther—earned the respect and admiration of the Israelite nation by playing significant roles in times of national crisis. Today women are still making a great contribution and a difference in their marriage relationships and to society on a whole.

"I do not need you to take care of me." Marva glared at Steve as she sauntered away. She felt stifled by all the attention from him. She had taken care of herself since she left home at 18 and now she was 39 years old. Why did Steve think she needed protection?

Over and over again Steve had said that women were the weaker vessel and needed men to take care of them. Where was he or any other men all these years when she was taking care of herself?

Can she ever get used to the idea that she is no longer on her own and that in another month she would be married?

Is she biting off more than she can chew? Why does she feel so trapped?

As you plan to enter this life of marriage, whether male or female, God has made you to be a complimentary lover. Recognize your role in the marriage and seek for ways to affirm the beauty and uniqueness of your spouse and find ways to celebrate and complement each other's strength. If husbands will continue to love and cherish their wives, God will use women to make a difference for their families, churches, and communities at large. If wives will acknowledge the gift that their husbands bring to the union and honor, respect and compliment him they will minimize differences and build on their strengths and grow healthy loving families.

A Weaker Vessel? Ask Jesus!

Many people say that because Jesus was not married, He did not really have a full view of women. It is true that

Jesus was not married, but if a man waits until marriage to gain a full appreciation of women, then he has waited too long! Even though Jesus was never married, He grew up in a loving relationship cultivated by His earthly parents, Joseph and Mary. He lived with his sisters and learned much about women from them. Jesus showed a great love for women and He demonstrated that throughout His earthly ministry.

Jesus was able to retain the best of the Hebrew tradition and, yet, cut away some of the rigid structure that restricted it. He was able to do the same toward women. Without radically changing their roles, Jesus enlarged and transformed women's possibilities for a full life. His manner and teachings elevated their status and gave them an identity and a cause.

The way Jesus dealt with women is as significant as His teachings about women. At the risk of censure from a male-oriented society, Jesus talked to women, responded to their touch, healed them, received their emotional and financial support, and used them as main characters in His stories. Jesus saw women as persons. Martha wanted Jesus to make Mary help with the serving duties, but Jesus affirmed Mary's choice to learn as a disciple. Women of that day could not be disciples or rabbis, but Jesus recognized their potential for intelligent thought and commitment (Luke 10:38-42).

In Mark 14:3-9, Jesus welcomed a woman's anointing His head as indicative of her understanding of His real mission. Instead of rejecting her public display or chiding her for extravagance, He commended her for her act of love. He treated her as a person of insight and feeling.

The woman at the well in Samaria is another example of Jesus seeing women as persons. Jesus would not have talked theology to her if He had related to her primarily as a woman or as a Samaritan. However, He saw her as a person, so He was not restricted in His interaction by her gender, culture, or race (John 4:1-42).

The woman, who had been caught in adultery, was treated as a person as well. Jesus did not condone her actions, but neither did He allow her to be subjected to a double standard by her male accusers. Jesus offered her new possibilities of living with His directive: "Neither do I condemn you. Go your way, and from now on do not sin again" (John 8:11).

Jesus involved women in His earthly ministry. Luke mentioned a group of women who traveled with Jesus as He journeyed from town to town (Luke 8:1-3). Among them were Mary of Magdala, Joanna, and Susanna. These women provided financial support for Jesus and the 12 apostles. Women also proclaimed the gospel. In His encounter with the Samaritan woman, Jesus revealed Himself as the Messiah. She immediately left and began telling people, "He told me everything I have ever done" (John 4:39b). Many Samaritans believed in Jesus because of her testimony.

Women were the first at the tomb after the Resurrection; and were the first to broadcast Jesus' victory over death (Luke 23:55-24:11). Matthew, Mark, and Luke called attention to the loyal women who participated in Jesus' Galilean ministry and who followed Him all the way to the cross and the tomb. They shared the greatest news: "He is not here but has risen" (24:5b).

As a master teacher, Jesus used parables to teach about the kingdom of God. He reached out to the women in His audience by telling stories about their life experiences as He did in Luke 15:8, 9: "Or suppose a woman has ten silver coins and loses one. Does she not light a lamp, sweep the house and search carefully until she finds it? And when she finds it, she calls her friends and neighbors together and says, 'Rejoice with me; I have found my lost coin'" (*NIV*). By using women in His parables, Jesus captured their attention and commitment, and offered them a place in the Kingdom.

God's seeking activity is the theme of two parables. The parable of the lost sheep begins, "What man of you . . ." and the parable of the lost coin begins, "What woman . . ." The woman looking for the lost coin represented God's activity in seeking the lost. In this parable, Jesus appealed to women through their housekeeping experiences. He elevated their experiences by likening them to God's activity. Jesus meant for women to identify with His mission, and to be involved in spreading the gospel. Again, Jesus used the life experience of women to illuminate an eternal truth.

The twin parables in (Luke 13:18-20) point to the way the kingdom of God grows. They taught that both women and men would be involved in Kingdom work.

Jesus spoke directly to the matter of treating a woman as a sex object. In the Sermon on the Mount, He redefined adultery to include a lustful look (Matthew 5:28). By making religion a matter of the heart instead of law, Jesus elevated women from sexual exploitation to full personhood. Because their lives were lived mainly in the roles of wife and mother, marriage and divorce were issues of great importance to women. Emotional, social, and financial securities were dependent upon their marriages. In Matthew 19:1-9, we are told that divorce is a testimony to the hardness of the human heart, not God's will. Jesus stated plainly that those men who were casually divorcing their wives were committing adultery. Responsive to the plight of women, Jesus offset the male bias toward divorce and strengthened marriage as a permanent union. (See Matthew 5:31, 32; 19:1-12; Mark 10:1-12; Luke 16:18.)

Jesus' parable of the five foolish and five wise maidens' hints at the way Jesus saw and dealt with women (Matthew 25:1-13).

He did not see women as inferior or superior, but simply as persons. He saw their potential, their sinfulness, their strengths and weaknesses, and He dealt with them directly. He elevated their status and strengthened their participation and influence in their world. Moreover, He treated them as friends and disciples.

Jesus Christ elevated the status of women and affirmed the roles of women in His day because He loved women with the same love He had for men. He observed the differences between the sexes, but He also recognized the equality of the sexes.

It behooves husbands, who are one in union with their wives, to show great love, respect and appreciation. Jesus, having so much love for women as the weaker vessel, demonstrated that care on the cross. While suspended between heaven and earth He called on John to take care of His mother Mary. "When Jesus therefore saw His mother, and the disciple standing by, whom he loved, he saith unto his mother, 'Woman, behold thy son!' Then saith he to the disciple, 'Behold thy mother!' And from that hour that disciple took her unto his own home" (John 19:26-27, KJV). At His resurrection the first messengers to announce His resurrection were women. Jesus used women in some very valuable and strategic position in the Kingdom.

It is important to note that the apostle Paul had a lot to say about women, and we will look at that in the next chapter. Many scholars argue that Paul had problems with women. Nevertheless, when we look at how he handled many issues surrounding women, we have to conclude that he also loved women and that a great portion of his support in ministry came from women.

Both narratives of Jesus and Paul have elevated women to the marriage table as complementary love partners. According the Jesus and Paul, both sexes are equal partners in the kingdom of God and marital relationships. Both husband and wife function as equals in life journey, one as pilot and the other as co-pilot interchangeable, by using their giftings, abilities and roles to reveal the image of God in society.

Discussion

1. How did Jesus open the boundaries for women?
2. What are the two views of women mentioned in the Old Testament?
3. Discuss Genesis 1:27 and Genesis 2:7-25.
4. Are women actually the weaker vessel? Why? Why not?
5. Did Jesus treat women as lesser human beings?

The Love Factor: Truths to Explore Before You Say, "I Do"

Chapter 4

Loving Who I Am

Scott looked at Megan and prayed softly. 'Lord please help her to recognize that in your eyes she is important and that you do not measure her based on her background"

Megan was embarrassed by the fact that her mother worked for Scott's family and because of that she felt that she was not good enough for him.

Scott's parents were okay with the relationship but Megan could not seem to get past the fact that her mother was their helper.

Should Scott move on or is there hope for this relationship?

Is this relationship doomed?

Marital love is all about sharing! True Christian love is all about giving. True marital love cannot be fully experienced until it is shared; and shared mutually! Marriage can only survive when each partner is willing to love who they are. However, we are going to ask a few questions, how can someone give love from a loveless life? Or how can someone give love until they have learnt how to love themselves?

A great loving marriage is, one that is built on a caring and sharing love from a healthy love reservoir. A healthy reservoir is one where each partner has a healthy view of self and others. As you think about finding a spouse, a life time companion, ask yourself, do I have a healthy love of self to share? Has my love grown enough so that I can share it with someone else? Healthy self-love comes through a personal relationship with God.

When individuals fail to establish their love for God, love of self and love for others, before marriage, they can compromise the structural integrity of the relationship thus threatening its stability and sustainability.

Let us **examine** these elements of a solid marital foundation.

Love for God

The love command in Deuteronomy 6:5, Love the LORD your God with all your heart and with all your soul and with all your strength, clearly indicates the profound appreciation and adoration that God requires. It also indicates that, as it relates to our affection and emotions, God is to be given priority. This is critical because on this hinges all other expressions of our love and devotion. The reality is that loving others adequately is evidence of love for God; love for God is demonstrated by love for the other.

Knowing what God requires and desiring to fulfill His will at all times becomes the deal breaker for many couples experiencing marriage deadlock. Had some couples observed this critical element prior to marriage, their relationship could have been saved.

1 John 4:20-21 provides our support for this position. John says:

> "If anyone says, "I love God," yet hates his brother, he is a liar. For anyone who does not love his brother, whom he has seen, cannot love God, whom he has not seen. 21 And he has given us this command: Whoever loves God must also love his brother."

The above verse is telling couples that they must devote themselves to unrestrained love for God, which removes hatred of brothers. This should involve their entire being, intellect, emotion and spirit. It was stated that love for God is demonstrated by love for our partners. However, this love finds expression in loving the other person correctly and love for the other is to be congruent to love for self. This is achieved as we commit ourselves to Him in submission and obedience.

Ones love and commitment to God is therefore reflected in the relationship. It is a critical foundational element; excluding uncompromised commitment to God from the relationship is a recipe for disaster. This leads us to our second foundational element for healthy self-love: love for others.

Love for others

The notion of love for the other is fundamental to Scripture. The Bible implies at least three compelling reasons for loving one another. Firstly, we are all created in the image of God. Secondly, this reality establishes our equality before God. In addition to that, the Bible teaches the universal fatherhood of God which therefore presupposes the universal brotherhood of man (Acts 17:26 - From one man he made every nation of men that they should inhabit the whole earth...) These three compelling realities urge our appreciation for the other in a most significant way and provide the Spirit-filled Christian couple with amazing security.

One may ask however, "how do we demonstration love for others appropriately without denying ourselves in some significant way? This question is eloquently answered by the following biblical injunctions:

1. Love your neighbour **as yourself** (Lev 19:18; Matt 19:19; Matt 22:37-39; Rom 13:8-10; Gal 5:14-15;)
2. Husbands ought to love their wives **as their own bodies** (Eph. 5:28)
3. Do to others **what you would have them do to you** (Matt 7:12)

These love commands indicate that without a proper appreciation of self, one cannot properly value the other. It is interesting to note that the injunctions seem to present 'self-love' as the paradigm for 'other love,' neighbor or partner. The neighbor is to be loved 'as self.' The wives are to be loved as the husband's 'own body.' In other words, the care that a husband has for his personal comfort should be consistent with that which he displays toward his wife.

It is further noted that not only should the neighbor be loved as one's own self and the wife be loved as the husband's own body, but that our actions toward others should be motivated by that which we would desire them to do to us. We should treat our partners in a manner similar to that which we desire of them.

The key lies in our understanding that loving the self appropriately offers the prototype for proper love for others. This is huge for a Spirit-filled Christian couple. Understanding this and appropriating it in a marriage can make all the difference. It would be the antidote for the ills that plague marriages: cheating, lying, abuse, deception, and selfishness.

The crucial question that may be asked is how is this accomplished in an age characterized by rapid change, narcissism, selfishness and individualism? It is only possible when couples allow the Holy Spirit to lead their lives.

Love of self

It is clear that it is absolutely critical for individuals to personally understand the order of love, if they are going to be able to appropriate the right kind of love to their neighbours. This understanding of loving self in relation to neighbour and loving neighbour in relation to self is the key to a better appreciation of self and others. Loving self authentically in our post-modern culture that's characterized by individualism, narcissism, greed, and selfishness does require consideration, but we cannot do it justice here.

To help us appreciate the love command, we need to look at two of the love commands in Scripture which seem to suggest that self-love is a model of love for others. The oft reiterated, love your neighbour as yourself, does not stand alone in this category. Men are instructed in Ephesians 5:28 to love their wives as their own bodies.

If we do not understand self-love, we will be our own archenemy. We will inadvertently relate to our partner and others based on our perception and our realities. Consequently, others will know the value we've placed on ourselves and treat us accordingly. Therefore, it must be repeated that loving self appropriately provides the paradigm for proper love for others, one's partner being the most significant. Healthy love of self must first be attained before we can truly love others. It can only be achieved when we make God's love our number one.

This love model was a command given in Deuteronomy to the Jews and later repeated in the New Testament church.

However, I need to emphasize that this was not new in Biblical practice.

In the Genesis account of creation, we see this model exemplified in the first human couple. When God made Adam and Eve, in Genesis 1:25-28; 2:21-15, He created them with a perfect love for God, self and others.

Genesis 3:8 tells us that God came walking in the garden talking with Adam in the cool of the day. It is clear from this statement that Adam had a relationship with God, so much that He could identify his voice. He had a wonderful relationship with God.

Adam also had a perfect love for himself. He was pleased with whom he was created to be; he was comfortable in himself and he embraced his role as the gardener of Eden. Adam appreciated his purpose and function in life as the custodian of paradise and all that God had put him in charge of. He was so comfortable with himself and appreciated others so much that when God presented Eve to him as his wife, he quickly acknowledged her as his equal companion and helpmate. He was not mindful of sharing his life and service with another person. He took her as his wife and the two became one.

Sin is the culprit that marred the perfect love relationship between God, self and others. The second Adam's (Jesus Christ) death and resurrection has provided a way to restore that broken love relationship. Today, those of us who have accepted Jesus Christ as Savior and Lord and have allowed the Holy Spirit to continually fill our lives daily will live in a wonderful relationship of love with God, self and others.

When there are problems with the proper understanding of the love command; to love self, it has the tendency to spill over in faulty Biblical marital roles. Such was the problem in the Corinthians church that still exists today.

Reading through the narrative of Corinthians we found a group of women who could not handle the new reality that was restored to them through the message of the gospel. They were given a voice to speak and share but some abused this change by usurping their husband.

Some women who were not prepared for their new freedom may have responded to the Gnostics who denied all sexual differences. These women started to behave in ways unbecoming to the gospel of Jesus Christ. They dominated discussions whether or not they had anything positive to contribute and they took pride in disagreeing with their husbands at public gatherings. In addition, some women even left their husbands. Paul indicated that the women were liberated to be fellow workers alongside men, but they missed Paul's point. Instead, they were determined to usurp the men's places and seize all the authority for themselves.

Paul called women back to order encouraging them to create balance in the church and the home. He reminded them that God is a God of order, and they ought to behave so that the cause of Christ might be furthered rather than scandalized. Thus, in the Corinthians' culture of that time, Paul demanded that women should wear veils, wear their hair long (1 Corinthians 11), keep quiet during discussions in worship services (v. 14), and refrain from teaching (1 Timothy 2). At first glance, it appears Paul was out to suppress women. In fact, his letters suggest that he was deeply moved by their general ignorance and immaturity. However, at other times he praises God for their service in the church, naming eight women (seven, if Junia is masculine) among the 26 church leaders in Romans 16. He calls Phoebe "deacon" (*diakonos*), (v. 1). Priscilla and her husband, Aquilla, were Paul's "fellow workers in Christ Jesus" (v. 3). Paul also names Apphia, Euodia, and Syntyche as church leaders (Philemon 2; Philippians 4:2).

Today's women are the subject of many questions and controversies in the church and this has led to questions and controversies in many marriages and families. As Christians turn to the Bible for guidance in responding to these questions, they must be careful not to focus on just one verse or passage. The total impact and message of the Bible should become the guiding spirit when answering questions.

The Old Testament clearly delegated the role of protector and loving leadership to the male. Woman was extolled for performing her important roles as wife and mother. On occasion she rose above those roles and led the Jewish nation in times of crisis. Husbands and wives need to know who they are and function appropriately.

The New Testament brings a different picture of women and wives. Jesus, and later Paul, elevated the status of woman so that she could be a full participant in the kingdom of God and marriage. However, she was urged to use her responsibility, as well as her freedom, to find her place in the body of Christ so that there would be a proper balance in the kingdom of God. The spirit of freedom and love in Christ belongs to both husbands and wives.

Thus, husbands should respect their wives, the gifts that God has placed in their lives, and treat them with love and as copartners in all aspects of life—ministry, business and home affairs. Jesus elevated and redeemed the status of women and men alike by His death on the cross. Therefore, husbands should love their wives as loving neighbors, as co-laborers and equal partners in life contrary to Romans laws and culture.

According to Roman law, the "House Codes" for family life in the New Testament (Ephesians 5:21-6:9; Colossians 3:18-4:1; and 1 Peter 2:18-3:7), should be interpreted against the background of the status of the family and the power of the head of the household in Roman society. Roman society, both legally and culturally, looked to the family as the primary unit of society. In early Roman law, and throughout the Roman period, the *paterfamilias* (head of the household) was the only fully legal person in the family. The family included those people who were considered "extended family"—wife, all unmarried children, married sons and their families, those persons adopted into the family, and slaves. Those persons lived under the *patria potestas*, or "absolute power," of the patriarchal head of the household. The *patria potestas* of the *paterfamilias* extended even to matters of life and death. A father was limited only by the constraints of the habit of consulting a family council or by the restraints of certain laws.

The father, for example, was the person who decided whether or not to allow a newborn infant to die. Such power flourished in the New Testament era and is borne out by the fact that one father had his son executed for participating in the Catiline Conspiracy of 62 B.C.

In early Roman times fathers could sell their children just as they could any other property. This absolute power of the Roman father included not only the persons directly descended from him, but also their personal property. In actuality, persons living under another's *patria potestas* owned nothing.

When daughters married, they moved into the power of another family's *patria potestas*. Upon the death of the *paterfamilias*, new families were created equal to all the sons living under his power (or grandsons, in the event their fathers had died). It was against this background that Paul's command to be subject to one another was given (Ephesians 5:21). This was a revolutionary word spoken to a society in which all were subject to the *paterfamilias*.

This command does face similar challenges today because the popular culture, many religions, and the media downplay and belittle or demoralize the status and roles of women. God was now saying to husbands that marital love relationships should be modeled after the example of Jesus Christ and the church. He was also saying that a husband's love for his wife would be wonderful if they lived a spirit-filled life as Paul indicated when he said, "And be not drunk with wine, wherein is excess; but be filled with the Spirit" (Ephesians 5:18, KJV).

The indwelling presence of God will supply the needed love for all husbands and wives to find complete fulfillment and happiness in marriage and it does not matter the times in which they are living.

Having a healthy loving view of oneself in a relationship will lead either partner to favor the other wisdom at most times for the good of marriage. The apostle Paul understood the power of self-love, so he moved ahead of his Jewish background and called for mutual submission between husbands and wives (Ephesians 5:21-33). Now, women were seeing some positive changes in their way of life, and God was making them a more integral part of His kingdom operation. The prevailing custom was for wives to be submissive. However, Paul reflected Jesus' concern that all relationships should reflect the grace extended by God. The grace given does provide the responsibilities for both husbands and wives to love each other and to follow the initial exhortation to submit to each other in love.

Pastor Johnson did not realize how much the decision that he made about his fiancé had affected her. How was he going to get her to reconsider calling off the wedding. He loved her! He could see the hurt in her eyes when she told him that she could not marry him under those conditions. She loved what she did and she would be very unhappy to just give that up because she was getting married.

After much discussion they decided to move forward with the wedding but only after counselling. Pastor Johnson was only too willing to comply and Megan went back to working with the kids.

The light that shone in her eyes again made him know he had done the right thing. Did Megan do the right thing by calling off the wedding?

In other passages Paul implied a hierarchy of submission. The sequence of this hierarchy extended from God, to Christ, to man, to woman, and finally to the child. The tone of this hierarchy was voluntary and self-sacrificing. Here again was a concession to order and not the ideal (1 Corinthians 11:2-16; 14:33-40; 1 Timothy 2:8-15).

Paul wrote responses to problems in the churches. Paul was concerned that the Christians should "give no offense to Jews or to Greeks or to the church of God" (1 Corinthians 10:32). He also wrote responses concerning specific problems in the churches and about the manner in which they should be handled.

Some of Paul's remarks do not have direct relevance to our day but have basic principles that are relevant to any time. For example, he spoke of meat offered to idols (Romans 14) and women wearing jewelry and braiding their hair (1 Timothy 2:8-12). Because of these principles, a Christian should take into account how his or her actions may influence others (1 Corinthians 8:13) and should do all things to the glory of God (1 Corinthians 10:31).

Paul's regard for women is equal to how he related to them. Paul welcomed women as co-laborers in the churches and commended them for their gifts and faithfulness (Romans 16:1, 3-5). Phoebe, Prisca, Lydia, and others were seen as partners in the gospel. To the Roman church Paul wrote, "I commend to you our sister Phoebe, a deacon of the church at Cenchreae" (Romans 16:1). He called Phoebe a "benefactor of many and of myself as well" (v. 2). Evidently, Paul relied on women to exercise their gifts (1 Corinthians 12) as a part of the body of Christ.

Women of today are as gifted as the women in Paul's day and should be allowed to function in the church as well as in their homes. Christ Jesus' coming fulfilled the law of God for the relationship between men and women and changed the family structure for the people of the church of God.

In Matthew, Jesus said, "Call no one your father upon earth, for you have one Father—the one in heaven" (23:9). The focus of family structure and lineage changed from the "earthly father" and was replaced by a lineage from "God the Father," which became accessible to anyone through Jesus Christ. Therefore, all who believe on Jesus become part of a broader family—God's family.

In the New Testament, marriage was founded on a bond of love experienced by both male and female. Women were no longer considered property by men, but instead were to be loved and nurtured (Ephesians 5:25); the roles of men and women were transformed by the love of Christ. The father was no longer the central figure of the family but was replaced by God the Father. The authority of the male was like the sacrificial-servant authority of Jesus Christ (Ephesians 5:25-33). All of this contrasts the arranged marriages in the Old Testament.

This mutual love commitment was a radical departure from the Old Testament marriage model. So, Paul called upon the New Testament church to base the marriage union on an equal and mutual sharing guided by love (1 Corinthians 7:4). The church is still living under the New Testament model, and we need to return to that model of mutual sharing guided by love rather than the faulty system of the world, which has polluted the church.

Marriages have a brighter future when couples start their relationship with a solid love in God. A God centered love always produces a healthy self-love which is shared in marriage.

Discussion

1. When women began to realize their freedom in Christ, how did they react?
2. In the book of 1 Corinthians, Paul lists some demands for women. Discuss his demands.
3. How did Paul feel about women as co-laborers in the church?
4. How do you feel about women as co-laborers in the church today and how? should that affect marriage?

Chapter 5

Submitted Lovers

Wives, be subject to your husbands as you are to the Lord (Ephesians 5:22).

Patricia hated the word submit. She was a preacher's kid and her dad had held the word "submission" over her mother's head for years. She promised herself that she would never allow any man to do that to her.

When Carl asked her to marry him, she made it quite clear that she had no intentions to submit to any man. She went out of her way to prove to him that he did not, and could not control her. Carl realized that this was a potential problem and told her that they need to see a counsellor for that before they got married.

He knew he loved her but he realized that this could turn out to be a serious problem if they did not take care of it before they got married. Patricia was reluctant to see the counsellor because in her mind there was nothing wrong with her.

One of the most controversial topics among the secular and religious worlds today is the issue of submission in marriage. It is a topic about which discussion must continue if marriage in the 21st century is going to rebound and reverse the high divorce rates.

In 1999, when the Southern Baptist Convention met in Oklahoma, they amended their declaration of beliefs to assert that a wife should, "submit graciously to the servant leadership of her husband." Because of this act, the secular media ridiculed the SBC. That declaration however, reaffirmed the Biblical genre of subjection in marriage as God's standard and order. Many female, liberal theologians, and feminists are speaking out against this Biblical order, but we must remember that God made the world, and He has the right to determine its order and its operation.

When we learn to follow God's careful design and order for His creation, we will experience divine harmony and earthly bliss. Wives are expected to submit to their husbands subsequent to the expression of their love. God designed that order. The problem with marriage is not with God's design and order marriage; it is because of man's abuse of God's order. If husbands are commanded to love their wives, husbands and wives must learn how to submit to each other in the Lord, and out of the same spirit, wives should follow the divine order of submission.

There have been different interpretations about the roles of husbands and wives in marriage. "There is neither male nor female, for you are all one in Christ Jesus" (Galatians 3:28). Human sexuality (maleness or femaleness) is an important aspect of human personality (Genesis 1:27).

The Bible provides considerable support for traditional roles of husbands and wives. It also provides examples of a variety of male/female roles. Martha performed the traditional role by preparing a meal for guests, but Mary played the non-traditional role of learner (Luke 10:38-42). Esau was a hunter, but Jacob liked to cook (Genesis 25:27-29). Leaders in the home and in society were generally men; but there were exceptions. Deborah was a judge (Judges 4-5), and Lydia was a merchant (Acts 16:14).

Priscilla and Aquilla seemed to have acted as a team in teaching Apollos (Acts 18:26). They also provided a meeting place for the church (Romans 16:3-5; 1 Corinthians 16:19). Even the ideal wife in Proverbs 31 exercised considerable creativity and initiative in far-ranging projects (Proverbs 31:16-20).

Different interpretations exist about authority and submission in marriage. On the one hand, there are those who believe that the husband, as head of the house, has a delegated authority from God over his wife. In this view, the wife's response is submission. On the other side, there are those whose model is the modern, democratic marriage in which the partners are equals in every sense of the word. In between are Christians who advocate a mutual submission in love as the ideal (Ephesians 5:21), but who also believe the husband has special leadership responsibilities. The key Biblical passages in this debate are Ephesians 5:21-32; Colossians 3:18, 19; 1 Peter 3:1-7. Advocates of strong male authority interpret these passages in light of the various Biblical passages reflecting the husband's authority (1 Corinthians 14:34, 35; 1 Timothy 2:11-14).

Those who take a more moderate view make the following points: Jesus' actions gave women a higher status than was accorded by the society of His day (Luke 8:1-3; 10:38-42; John 4:7-30), and Paul's more idealistic statements (Galatians 3:28) and actual practice (Acts 16:14, 15; Romans 16:3-6) indicate that his harder teachings may have been conditioned by specific situations in some first-century churches.

Mutual Submission in Love

The admonition to mutual submission in Ephesians 5:21 applies to all the relationships within the church (Ephesians 5:25-6:10) and in a Christian marriage (Ephesians 5:21-33). Both Paul's and Peter's use of submission refer to voluntary submission in a loving relationship, not the forced subjection to authority in a military organization. The Biblical references say to submit yourself to one another, not put the other person under your subjection (Ephesians 5:21, 22, 24; Colossians 3:18; 1 Peter 3:1). In this type of relationship, the husband's role as head is modeled after the self-giving of Christ (Ephesians 5:23, 25; Philippians 2:1-11; 1 Peter 3:7).

The Apostle Paul's passages on marriage, found in Colossians 3:18, 19; Ephesians 5:22, 23, and 1 Peter 3:1, speak of women being in submission to their husbands. It is therefore important to notice the significant role that the concept of submissiveness plays in the New Testament.

Before we conclude, it is important to state that nowhere in the Bible does submission in marriage mean inferiority. Christ submitted unto His parents (Luke 2:5 1) and the Father (1 Corinthians 15:28). The submission in these passages has to do with obeying one's calling, being subject to the demands of the office. Nowhere does it state that women are to be subject to men. However, in the position of wife, a woman is to lovingly submit herself to her husband's love, care and leadership. Submitting one to another, in the fear of God, (Ephesians 5: 21, KJV) emphasizes that members of Christ's body are fulfilling their calling.

Paul's call to submission is particularly important because in the next verse he specifically tells wives to submit to their own husbands. Submitting to one another does not involve being substandard; instead, it is the calling to serve each other in order to fulfill God's demands. Thus, Paul does not imply that women are deficient or inferior even when he reminds wives to submit to their husbands in Ephesians 5:22: "Wives, be subject to your husbands, as you are to the Lord"; and Colossians 3:18: "Wives, be subject to your husbands, as is fitting in the Lord."

Moreover, the focus is not so much on the wives and husbands as it is on the offices of wives and husbands as they relate to each other; not so much on the individuals involved but more on what is normal for marriage. In effect, Paul says, "Be wives as is fitting in the Lord," as the norm for marriage instructs. "Wives, submit to your husbands as to the Lord" (Ephesians 5:22, *NIV*); as the Lord God for requires of Christian couples.

The knowledge of marriage relations is especially striking when we see that in Ephesians 5:25 Paul immediately adds: "Husbands, love your wives, as Christ loved the church and gave himself up for her"; and in Colossians 3:19: "Husbands, love your wives, and never treat them harshly." Paul is saying, "Remember what Christ did for the church. The care that He showed is the care that you should share in your marriages."

Although the wives may have some legitimate grievances, the solution is neither running away nor a writ of divorce. Even as Paul instructs women to be good wives, he exhorts men to be good husbands. Both husbands and wives are to live up to their calling. She is to be a loving and submissive wife and he is to be a loving, caring, and gentle husband.

We must not conclude from these texts that women do not have to submit or love their husbands or that husbands do not have to love or care for their wives. That conclusion would be preposterous. Paul is calling both husbands and wives to be obedient to the standards for marriage, which involve mutual love and mutual submission. The equality of marriage is heightened even more when we recall that in

Christ's life, submission and love were synonymous to loving and serving. Christ emphasized the service concept of marriage in direct contrast to any of the other concepts in existence at that time. Six times in the synoptic gospels we read that the greatest must be the servant of all (Matthew 20:26-28; 23:11; Mark 9:3-5; 10:43, 45; Luke 9:48; 22:26, 27). Naturally then, Christ requires that husbands and wives submit to each other in love and thus obey the will of God.

First Peter 3:1 deserves mention because, in an indirect way, it confirms our contention that being in submission does not mean being "bossed around." Wives are to be in submission to their husbands so that if any man is an unbeliever, he can perhaps be won for Christ by the behavior of his wife. This submission however, does not entail authority to forbid wives from believing in Christ. Like Paul, Peter is calling wives and husbands to function as mandated.

Christianity should make it easier for a husband to love his wife. However, religion does not set the standard for love. God is love, and He establishes love and places it in an intimate union. He also places the responsibility of maintaining and sustaining that love on the shoulders of the husband, whether he is a Christian or not. Wives, according to Peter, are not to be show-offs or to play the role of "loose" women. Likewise, husbands are to act with understanding and to love their wives as vessels designed to be loved (1 Peter 3:7).

Husbands Role in Submission

What is the duty of the Christian husband? The Scriptures are clear in this regard. He is to live with his wife, and he is to understand and honor her with the highest esteem.

The Greek word *sunoikein* means to dwell with, to remain with—to reside with. Husbands are to remain with their wives and treat them with love knowing that they are heirs together of the same grace of life (1 Peter 3:7). Stibbs points out that *sunoikein* is a word that is often used in the Greek for sexual intercourse. It is similar to the Hebrew verb for "to know" which means that a man and woman know each other sexually. The point is that the husband is to dwell with his wife and with no one else. He is to dwell with her in purity, righteousness, and holiness, and not as an adulterer.

To dwell with his wife also means that the husband is not to be gone all of the time pursuing his own interests and hobbies. He will give up on his interests and hobbies at times to serve at home to meet the needs of his wife and children. A good husband dwells at home, he is close to his wife, and he is supportive of her in all aspects of life. The husband and wife are a team. They are as one body; one body that lives and moves together. This is not to do away with individuality, because individuality never has been and never will be the problem within a marriage. The problem with people will always be their attempts to deny self and sacrificially give themselves to their spouses. Husbands must always remember this: They are to live and move and have their being with their wives.

> *For this cause shall a man leave his father and mother, and cleave to his wife; and they twain shall be one flesh: so then they are no more twain, but one flesh. What therefore God hath joined together, let not man put asunder (Mark 10:7-9, KJV).*
>
> *And Adam said, "This is now bone of my bones, and flesh of my flesh: she shall be called Woman, because she was taken out of Man. Therefore shall a man leave his father and his mother, and shall cleave unto his wife: and they shall be one flesh" (Genesis 2:23, 24, KJV).*

Husbands are to live with their wives in knowledge. This is a fact that is too often ignored and neglected. However, the Scripture is clear; a husband is not to be ignorant in living with his wife. He is to know and understand:
1. The marriage relationship—what marriage is and what it is to be.
2. His wife—her nature and emotional makeup; what she needs and wants emotionally and spiritually; her strengths and weaknesses.
3. His duties—what the Word of God says.

A good husband submit himself to be a disciple of his wife; to study, know and understands his wife so he can meet her changing needs. He should not be prejudiced and inconsiderate, not blind and close-minded, not a detached and inconsiderate observer.

Husband submits himself to the Holy Spirit so he can know how to be the type of love he needs to give his wife on a daily basis. Without, the leading of the Holy Spirit, it will be very difficult for husbands to lead and love their wives. Why? A problem in marriage affects a woman differently than how it would a man. The husband needs the help of the Holy Spirit to see the problem beyond their view so that he can understand and administer the right solutions that will benefit both sexes.

Husbands are to honor their wives. The word *honor* (*timen*) means to value, to esteem, to prize, to count as precious. A husband is to count his wife a precious gem, a prize of extreme value. He is to highly esteem her. The husband is to honor his wife as the weaker vessel. By nature, the wife is more delicate. This means that the husband is:
1. To protect her.
2. To be the primary provider.
3. To assume leadership in the home.
4. To oversee the family and its welfare.

Husbands are to look after and care for their wives with warmth and tenderness, treating them in the most precious of spirits. *Husbands love your wives, even as Christ also loved the church, and gave himself for it* (Ephesians 5:25, KJV).

In God's eyes, men and women are joint (equal) heirs. The husband is to honor his wife as a joint heir of the grace of life. The husband is neither above the wife nor the wife above the husband. God has no favorites. Spiritual gifts and rights are given to wives and husbands equally. Women receive the spiritual gifts of God just as men do.

Failure to honor the wife hinders the prayers of the husband. God will not answer the prayers of any husband who dishonors his wife. God hears the sighs of the wife, not the prayers of a mean and domineering husband. God is going to hear the broken and contrite heart, not the prayers of the arrogant and dominating spirit. Both husband and wife must love one another and live as God says to live, both fulfilling their duty to one another, if they wish God to answer their prayers.

> *If I regard iniquity in my heart, the Lord will not hear me (Psalm 66:18, KJV).*
>
> *But your iniquities have separated between you and your God, and your sins have hid his face from you, that he will not hear (Isaiah 59:2, KJV).*

This does not mean that the husband should always control. Paul stressed the equality of the roles. Recognizing their places as wife and husband, the partners must do everything in accordance with the Biblical truths. Thus, Paul stated that even as the church is subject to Christ and she is not her own savior, so a wife is not to forget her role of wife, but she is to be wife to her husband in everything (Ephesians 5:23).

Look at Paul's teaching on the mutuality of marriage in 1 Corinthians 7:3, 4: "The husband should give to his wife her conjugal rights, and likewise the wife to her husband. The wife does not rule over her own body, but the husband does, likewise the husband does not have authority over his own body; the wife does." Here it is spelled out for us. There must be mutuality in marital sexual relationship in order for love to be fully experienced. Wives and husbands should give themselves to their spouses. They should be motivated by the other's desire rather than how they are feeling at the moment.

There are many different ways to express love. Although there are different roles established for the sexes in different cultures of the world, the command of God for man to love his wife crosses every culture and age. The church must now look at theology through some broader views such as the feminist, woman, black, poor, and the oppressed to balance out the Anglo-male, middle-class view of theology. The church is challenged to remain consistent with the bible by creating a mosaic theology that does justice to all of mankind. It is difficult to look at submission without looking at the incarnation of Jesus because it epitomizes the submission and headship concept. In Philippians 2:1-11, we find the incarnation of Jesus Christ the truest representation of love and submission in action. If marriages are going to last, wives must practice the submissiveness demonstrated and practiced by Jesus Christ, and husbands must practice a loving leadership as God did with Jesus while He lived in this world.

Jesus Christ is the supreme example of submissiveness and humility. This passage says that Jesus Christ is God, yet He humbled and submitted Himself and became man. Jesus Christ is the person who dwelt in all the glory of perfection, but He humbled Himself and came to this corruptible world that was filled with selfishness, greed and death. Jesus took an enormous step down to become a man. It will take the mind of Christ dwelling in a wife in order for her to submit to her husband, just as it will for the husband to love his wife according to the Biblical standard.

When Paul made the statement in Philippians 2:6, "Who being in the form of God did not consider it robbery to be equal with God" (KJV), he made it clear that Christ is of the very nature of God. Hence, Christ was fully God as He was fully man.

Jesus Christ is of the being of God. The word *being* (*huparchon*) means "existence," what a person is within and without. It is the very essence of a person—what he is inside—that cannot be changed. It is who a person is and all that he is. Jesus Christ is in the form of God. The word *form* (*morphe*) means "the permanent, constant being of a person." In contrast, it means the fleeting, outward form of a person that is always changing. For example, a man is always changing (*schema*) in looks because of age and fashion. However, his manhood (*morphe*) never changes.

In the incarnation, Jesus Christ emptied Himself and became a man. He, who existed, in eternity and perfection, in glory and majesty, and in dominion and power, stepped down and became a man. But more than this, He who was the Lord and Master of the universe—who deserved all honor and service of all living creatures—took upon Himself the form of a servant. He became the servant of men—not only of God.

Jesus Christ made Himself of no reputation. That is, He emptied Himself. The word *emptied* (*ekenosen*) means "to completely empty." It is the picture of pouring water out of a glass until it is empty—dumping everything until it is all removed. Matthew Henry made a brief but excellent statement about this fact: "He emptied Himself, divested Himself of the honors and glories of the upper world, and of His former appearance, to clothe Himself with the rags of human nature" (Matthew Henry Study Bible 2011).

When a wife submits to her husband in love, she is not giving up her essence, or personhood. She is simply submitting herself to her husband in love, knowing that he will love and care for her, and that together they will be able to maximize each other to fulfill their potential. When a wife fully submits to her husband and the husband fully gives unto his wife, that marriage will be modeled and emulated. If Christ, being God, could willingly submit to His father in love, then the same Christ, who indwells us and demonstrated how to submit and to love, will lead us to fulfill our roles. All we have to do is allow Him to guide us.

There is submission and unity in the Godhead. Christ submitted to the Father and willingly came to earth to die for mankind (Mark 14:36). The Holy Spirit came and fulfilled the promise of the Father (John 14:26). The Father submits to the advocacy of His Son as He intercedes for the church (John 17:9-26).

Submission Model in the Godhead

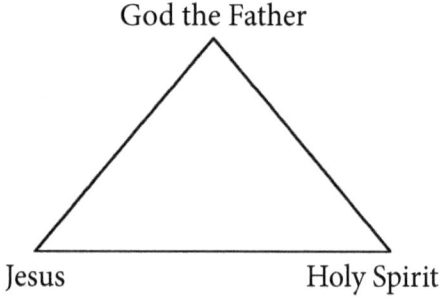

Figure 1.

In Figure 2, the husband submits to Christ, the Holy Spirit infills him. In love the husband leads his wife, and she willingly submits and follows his leading. When the wife submits to her husband, she is also submitting to the divine design of Christ's norm for marriage. Wives are required to submit to their own husbands as the husbands submit to God (Ephesians 5:21).

Submission of Husband and Wife in God

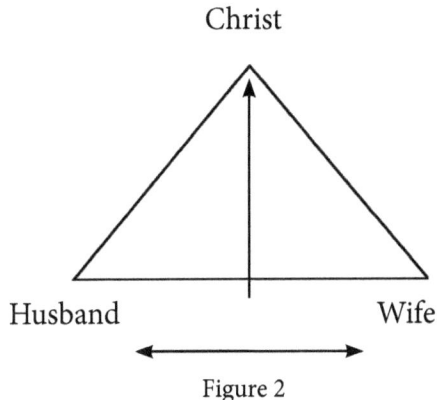

Figure 2

Marriage requires mutual submission between husbands and wives as they also submit to Christ, the head of the church—the source of the creation of mankind.

A Spirit-filled husband will submit to Christ and out of his allegiance to Christ will pour forth his love to his wife. The wife in response submits to Christ and to the loving care and leadership of her husband. Love and submission work harmoniously as both submit to the divine leadership of Christ. There should not be one without the other.

Discussion

1. What are the traditional rolls of husbands and wives? Discuss.
2. Discuss some of the different interpretations about authority and submission in marriages.
3. Discuss how Christianity makes it easier for husbands and wives to function as a couple.

Chapter 6

Companionship Lovers

"I am the head of my house" Raymond shouted, "and as the head, once we are married, what I say goes. Marva rolled her eyes and groaned. What was she getting herself into? This had become Raymond's mantra ever since they got engaged. "You better start practicing how to follow my lead from now" he continued.

Marva had no problem with her husband being the head of the household. However, she felt that Raymond was totally missing the point.

What was she to do?

Probably one of the most misinterpreted and an abused issue in marriage is the meaning and application of headship. If a husband is to love his wife, as the Bible requires, he must first understand his God-given position of headship. He must understand it through careful study of the Word of God and not through his cultural, theological, sociological presuppositions. Wives must also know what to expect from their husbands, as heads of their lives, based on the Word of God, and not by those same predispositions.

The headship concept was referred to in an earlier chapter, but I would like to discuss it in more detail now. As we know, the head is the uppermost part of the body, and is considered to be the seat of life. It is interpreted figuratively as first, top, or chief.

The Jewish notion was that the heart was the center or seat of the intellect. It was often used to represent the whole person (Acts 18:6). The word *head* often has the meaning of "source" or "beginning," and it designates one in authority—the foremost person. A husband is the "head of the wife" (Ephesians 5:23).

A distinctive theological use of the word *head* was seen in the New Testament concept of the "headship" of Christ. Christ is the "head" (*kephale*) of His church and the church is His "bride" (Ephesians. 5:23-33). In His role as "head," Christ enables the church to grow, knits her into a unity, nourishes her by caring for each member, and gives her strength to build herself up in love (Ephesians 4:15-16). Not only is Christ "head" of the church, but He is also "head" of the universe (Ephesians 1:22) and of every might and power (Colossians 2:10).

The divine influences on the world result in a series: God is the head of Christ, Christ is the head of man, man is the head of woman, and as such husbands are to love and care for their wives as Christ does the church—His bride (1 Corinthians 11:3). This theological use of the word may be an extension of the Old Testament use of the word *head* for the leader of the tribe or community or may be a reaction to early Gnostic tendencies.

If we conclude from this passage that man is superior to woman, we must likewise conclude that Christ is subordinate to God. The church has denied the second conclusion, and it is time she emphatically rejects the first.

Paul's meaning rests on the word *head*. Whatever the exact meaning of headship is in 1 Corinthians, it is apparent that an important aspect of the concept is prominent. Head does not mean "lord," but is virtually synonymous with "beginning" or "origin." This reading does, however, make excellent sense in all of its New Testament occurrences. The focus is on the derivation of woman from man.

The passage in 1 Corinthians says in negative terms: "Without Christ from out of whom and in relation to whom man exists, there is no man. Without man from out of whom and in relation to whom woman exists, there is no woman. Without God from out of whom and in relation to whom Christ exists, there is no Christ" (1 Corinthians 11:11, 12). This passage says the same thing as Genesis 2:21, 22, 24 about the place and nature of woman; she has no existence in herself, but then neither has man. She can only be defined in relation to man.

Later Paul declares that man cannot be fully man without woman, and both can only be defined in relation to Christ and through Christ to God. Paul is defending the male/female distinction without claiming that women are inferior. Having made his point, Paul adds that failing to wear veils, which was a cultural practice in Corinth, during prophecy and prayer, signified a woman's refusal to act as a woman and demonstrated rebellion against God and man. To appear without a veil in Corinth was unwomanly and shameful. At the same time, non-Christian Corinthian women apparently removed their veils during religious observances. Paul also wanted to distinguish the conduct of Christian women from that of pagan worshipers. He noted ironically, that if women did not wear veils, they might as well shave off their hair (reputedly the custom of prostitutes of the time).

Today, neither a veil nor the length of a woman's hair suggests that she accepts or rejects her role as a woman. Neither one distinguishes Christian from non-Christian conduct. Instead, modern life demands that we guard against blurring the sexual distinction and that we develop a distinctive Christian lifestyle in other ways.

Christianity teaches that God and Christ are equal in the Godhead. The Genesis account of the creation of Adam and Eve revealed that they were created equally. In the Second Adam, Christ's equality was restored. However, in light of the God-created order of the family, man is the head, because woman came from the man. Therefore, as the head he is responsible for the welfare of his wife and family. Husbands are responsible for providing a loving environment for the well-being of his wife and children, just as Christ, the head of the church, provides for the loving environment and well-being of the church. It is clear from Scripture that man is the head. However, husbands need to remember that their wives are the "neck that turns the head." Marriage is a partnership, and we need to function in our roles. It is out of this loving headship that wives shine as the glory of their husbands

Discussion

1. Based on the Word of God, what should wives expect from husbands?
2. How is the word *head* used in the New Testament in relation to Christ and the husbands?

Chapter 7

Loves Grandeur

Dameon paused and looked at himself in the mirror. He smiled when he remembered the way he used to dress before he met Monica.

He loved the fact that she was not forceful about it; neither did she try to embarrass him as other women had done. Instead she gently and gradually taught him how to dress and now he finally got it. He was confident in selecting his own outfits for any occasion.

Today was their wedding and he had to admit he was looking pretty sharp; he was thankful for Monica's coaching.

Isn't it great to know that women are the glory of men? Without having the right women in their lives, men would surely be a pathetic bunch! Most wives help husbands with their dressing and some of the finer points of life so that when they stand alongside them, their presences take husbands to another level. I am not sure that this is what the author of Corinthians had in mind when he spoke about the glory of man, but it does not minimize the truth that women make men look good or some better.

In 1 Corinthians 11 (KJV), Paul expands his argument by asserting that a woman ought to cover her head (v. 6), and a man "ought not to cover his head because man is the image and glory of God: but the woman is the glory of the man" (v. 7). It would be wrong if we stopped at this point. He rephrases the argument to avoid misunderstandings.

Paul continues, "Nevertheless, neither is the man without the woman, neither the woman without the man, in the Lord. For as the woman is of the man, even so is the man also by the woman; but all things of God" (v. 11, 12).

A careful reading of the entire passage indicates that Paul is not defending the superiority of man over woman but stressing their "bi-unity," mutuality, and dependence even in their differences. The phrase in verse 9, "the woman for the man" does not mean that woman was made to serve man. In terms of Genesis 2:18, it underlines God's intention that woman was made to be a helper and partner for man. Although the full meaning of glory is not yet clear and is difficult to comprehend, it certainly carries the connotation of the Hebrew word for glory (*kabod*), which means "weight."

When a man has weight, He has worth, importance, and honor (glory). To describe a person as the glory of someone else is to define that person in terms of the one he reveals. When a husband is a man of God, he has weight and importance; he is the glory of God. He is a living demonstration or image of his Maker; therefore, he will love his wife as Christ loves the church, and he will be willing to lay down his life for his wife as Christ laid down His life for the church, His bride. Husband, as the glory of God, reflects an image of God as he demonstrates in his care, love, respect and honor for all that God put under his influence. In a similar way, when a woman has weight and importance, and the glory of man. When husbands and wives realize that their existence is impossible without each other, only then can mankind (male and female) be fulfilled and satisfied.

Another difficult portion of 1 Corinthians 11 is the sentence, "For this cause ought the woman to have power on her head because of the angels" (v. 10, KJV). The "power" or "authority" (*exousia*) that a woman is to have on her head is commonly thought to be a sign of the power of the man to whom she must be subjected. However, this interpretation has no philosophical support. In no other Scripture passage does *exousia* mean "powerlessness," as this interpretation suggests. Furthermore, the context of the verse offers no support for this view. It makes better sense to think of *exousia* as a sign of woman's own authority. The phrase "because of the angels" emphasized that God was indeed present because angels represented God's presence in worship services.

A wife is not powerless. She has delegated power that is to be used in the marriage union according to God's design in collaboration with her husband. A Christian husband should demonstrate a life of love to reflect the glory and the image of God, and the wife should use her power to add significance to her husband and ultimately exalt their marriage.

Therefore, when they stand together at home or in public places, their presence should display the glory of God and demonstrate a loving relationship to those who look at them. As the glory of God was seen upon Moses in a physical way, so should the glory of a happy marriage union be seen in physical ways at home and in the public lives of each couple?

We have covered many issues about women in the Bible, but there is one more crucial issue, and we will focus on that in the next chapter.

Discussion

1. In what ways can wives be the "glory of their husbands"?
2. Is a woman powerless in the marriage union?
3. In what ways does she have power?
4. How does a husband show forth the glory of God in his marriage union?

Chapter 8

Love Busters

Earl was literally afraid of Judith. He had no idea she had such a bad temper and in the weeks since they got engaged it seems to have gotten worst.

He wondered what could have happened for her to react like this whenever she did not get her own way. She would literally turn into someone he did not recognize.

Nobody from church would ever believe him if he said it. She was such a sweet person at church that everybody liked her.... but he had gotten to know the Judith outside of church and it was not pretty

Judith also recognized that she was beginning to behave just like her mum did towards her father. She hated the way her mum treated her dad and she was doing the same thing to Earl.

They needed help and they needed it fast!

The 21st Century seems to have introduced the world to some very wonderful inventions and advancement, cure to many medical ailments, but with it brings with it a new reality that is destroying our culture and marriage. This new reality is called Bullying.

Bullying has become pattern of behavior that is routine practices in many relationships. It is an imbalance of social, physical, mental, spiritual or other power involving a person, marriage, group or organization. The culture of bullying is seen in daily activities and the ways people relate to each other.

Bully is a learnt behavior. It is a winner/loser way of thinking. It also encourages domination and submission. A careful analysis of these traits should cause all children of God to agree that none of the foregone traits are compatible with Christian marriage. But you will soon see that marriage is not exempt from bullying.

When most people think of bullying, they think of the behavior that occurs between children, either at school, in the neighborhood or through the internet or social media. While this is the most common type of bullying, there are other types of bullying that do exist. For instance, spouse bullying is a real problem in many marriages. It is worse in some cultures.

Spouse bullying is a love buster and it must be addressed in premarital preparation and within the church community. Today, it is no longer just husbands battering wives; it now includes wives battering/abusing their husbands. Whether via the wife or husband, battering is a love buster that should never enter into a marriage; much less a Christian marriage. We will come back to this evil practice latter!

Jenny and I would like to look at a few more Love Busters that has been around for eons, but was never carefully studied, addressed and categorized until Dr. Willard F. Harley did his research and wrote about his findings.

Harley says he calls all the ways that spouses are inconsiderate of each other's feelings Love Busters. They are Love Busters because they destroy the love that a husband and wife have for each other.

In Dr. Harley's research he found out that there are six main ways couples behave or act that creates Love Busters:

1. Selfish Demands
2. Disrespectful Judgments
3. Angry Outbursts
4. Annoying Habits
5. Independent Behavior
6. Dishonesty

Harley believes that the first three Love Busters are automatic responses. These are thoughtless techniques that spouses use to try to get what he/she wants from the other. When a spouse request is not granted, that spouse will regularly retreat to making demand such as ("I don't care how you what you are doing or how you are feeling – just do it or else!"). Further if that threat didn't get the job done, then the spouse will advance to more lethal measures. They may say things like ("If you had any sense, and were not so lazy and selfish, you would do it"). And it gets worse if this attack fails. Here comes the angry outburst. Punishment! ("You will pay for not meeting my request.") If nothing else kills a love quicker, these love busters will.

Marriage is not about making your ways and wishes a priority; it is about reaching out to meeting the needs of your spouse. Dr. Harley concludes that when a spouse practices these three Love Busters, it destroys the love that they have for each other.

The fourth Love Buster, Annoying Habits, is behavior that is repeated without much thought that it bothers your spouse. As you look at your life now, if you see any of these three behaviors seek counseling early. If you want to stay in love with each other, these habits, as innocent as you think they are, withdraw from your Love Bank instead of making deposits.

The fifth Love Buster, Independent Behavior, is what Jenny and I consider the most dangerous of all six. When an individual place his or her own interest above the interest of a spouse, they are driving a nail into their coffin. To ignore the feelings and interests of the other spouse is sure relationship death. When you say "I do" in a marriage vow it removes the priority of individual behavior to couple behavior. Individual behavior should never trump the couple's best interest.

Harley's final Love Buster is, Dishonesty! If you know that you have the tendency to be dishonest, this is the time to address it and get help. Dishonesty should never have any place in your marriage. Dishonesty destroys intimacy. It is easily discovered. Dishonesty greatly affects couple's emotional closeness. This should serve as a great warning, "If you or your spouse has a tendency to lie or distort the truth, chase that bad habit out of your marriage before it ruins everything." (97)

An understanding of Harley's six Love Busters reveals that they are all anchored in selfishness! So too is wife or husband abuse; it is anchored in selfishness. In the case of spousal abuse, one party resolves to use the only method they know to handle their inner struggles and issues by taking it out on the other. Sooner or later without addressing this issue, it can lead to death or divorce. Marriage is designed to provide healing for selfishness and build oneness. However, that goal is only possible when each spouse becomes totally open to God and to each other; seeking professional help where and when needed.

Bullying: Love's Silent Killer

Wife or husband abuse is a major social issue for today's society as well as for the church. Family violence, while common around the world, is not a universal problem. It is rare or entirely absent in 15 percent of societies.

Levinson states that the factors that influence low, or no, family violence include monogamous marriages, economic equality between the sexes, equal access to divorce by men and women, the availability of alternative caretakers for children, and frequent and regular intervention by neighbors and family in domestic disputes. Society, and the church, cannot ignore the abuse of women in our parishes, communities, and, indeed, the country. Loving husbands need to raise the standards for husband/wife relationships and should challenge men who beat their wives to cease the abusive behavior.

In 1985, husbands or boyfriends killed over 1,300 women. That was 30 percent of the total homicides of females. Wives or girlfriends killed 6 percent of the male homicide victims. Approximately 37 percent of pregnant females across class, race and educational lines are physically abused. Four million women are severely assaulted each year. Over onethird of assaults to women involve severe aggression such as punching, kicking, choking, or the use of a knife or gun.

Kilgore says that from onefifth to onethird of all women are physically assaulted by a partner in their lifetimes. Approximately 95 percent of battered victims are women and 21 percent of all women who use the hospital emergency surgical services are abuse victims. The rate of injury to battered women surpasses that of car accidents and muggings combined.

There are no exterior signs, no "marks of Cain," to distinguish the batterer or the rapist. Abusers cut across all ethnic, religious, cultural and professional lines, and they are from all socioeconomic groups. This fact is a strong and sobering rebuke to those who think that batterers are only in poor urban areas or of a certain color or class. If you grew up in a home where physical and spousal abuse occurred, you are exposed to this evil and it is possible for you to carry that trait into your new relationship. Pre-marriage preparation should include ways of helping you overcome these traits before it starts and become another cycle.

The Cycle of Abuse

The cycle that I am describing, first developed by Lenore Walker in her book *Battered Women*, has three phases—the tension-building phase, the acute-battering incident and the kind-and-contrite loving behavior.

Walker believes that stress feeds the tension-building phase. She states that the more stress you are under, the shorter the phase lasts, and the abuse that follows is more severe. This phase can last anywhere from days to several years. It is like a pressure cooker being placed over an open flame without a release valve. As the batterer and the battered woman sense the escalating tension during this first phase, it becomes more difficult for their coping techniques to work. Each becomes more frantic. The man increases his possessive smothering and brutality, his attempts at psychological humiliation become more barbed, his verbal harangues longer and more hostile. He hovers around her barely giving her room to breathe on her own. Tensions between the two become unbearable.

The acute-battering incident phase is the time when the batterer lashes out at his victim. Batterers always blame the women for causing the blow up. They also claim that the stressful nature of their lives needs to come to an end. This is the phase when tremendous physical injuries can and do occur. When the acute attack is over, initial denial and disbelief that it has really happened usually follows. Both the batterers and their victims find ways of rationalizing the seriousness of such attacks. If there has been physical violence the battered woman will often minimize her injuries. For example, a woman, whose husband tried to choke her with a metal chain, reported that she was grateful that she only had marks around her neck, rather than cuts from the chain breaking the skin. In minimizing the attack, a woman might say, "He only said that because he was angry. If he had been his normal self, he wouldn't have said it."

The final phase, the kind-and-contrite loving behavior, is loaded with promises that further verbal assault and physical injuries will never happen again. It is this phase that generally keeps the relationship together and keeps both partners in denial. He enjoys being relieved of the inner stress—certain it will never happen again—and she enjoys the special attention that her battering husband gives her. The couple that lives in a violent relationship becomes a symbiotic pair, each so dependent on the other that when one attempts to leave both lives become drastically affected. It is during phase three—when the loving kindness is most intense—that this symbiotic bonding really takes hold. They fool themselves into believing that together they can battle the world. The sense of overdependence and overreliance upon each other is obvious in each phase of the cycle. The bonding aspects of it, however, are laid down during phase three.

Jones indicated, in *Next Time She'll Be Dead*, that while it is important to understand the cycle of abusive behavior on the part of men who batter women, battering must not be seen as isolated or random attacks on the victims. Ann Jones puts responsibility where it rightfully belongs—in the laps of the batterers. It is vital to understand that battering is not a series of isolated blow-ups. It is a process of deliberate intimidation intended to coerce the victim to do the will of the victimizer. The batterer is not just losing his temper, not just suffering stress, and not just manifesting insecurity or spontaneous reaction. He or she is usually provoked by something the victim does, or by his/her own inability to control his anger. Therapists who work with batterers agree that these are often-used excuses; yet, we all know aggrieved, insecure, stressed-out people with meager interpersonal skills who lose their temper without becoming violent. It is these thoughts that provide a public excuse and deceive a battered woman into giving her batterer another chance to be the socalled real, nonviolent man within.

Abuse: A Product of Social Learning

O'Leary states that social-learning-theory proponents reject the notion that aggression is an inner drive. They argue, instead, that aggression is both learned and practiced in a social context. This suggests that a combination of contextual and situational factors cause family violence. Some contextual factors are individual characteristics, couple characteristics, and societal characteristics.

Pagelow, Kalmuss and Strauss all believe there is considerable evidence that individuals who have observed, or perhaps experienced family violence in their childhood homes, are not likely to be involved in violent behavior in marital relations. However, Rita-Lou Clarke indicates in her book, *Pastoral Care of Battered Women*, that when we look at the extent and pervasiveness of wife abuse, we must conclude that it is not a problem of marital maladjustment or personality maladjustment of a few.

Patriarchy is the manifestation and institutionalization of male dominance over women and children in the family and the extension of male dominance over women in society in general. Gerda Lerner, in his work *The Creation of Patriarchy*, examines patriarchy in its wider meaning. He states that it implies that men hold power in all the important institutions in society, and that women are deprived of access to such power. It does not imply that women are totally powerless or totally deprived of rights, influence, and resources; but in most cases, women as a group and some men have less power, less influence, and fewer resources.

At the heart of the patriarchal system is the belief that men should control and dominate women. The common law in England gave the husband the right to beat his wife—providing the switch was not bigger than his thumb. Hence, the proverbial "rule of thumb."

Lenore Walker lists common characteristics of battered women that the church and its leadership must know (for the record, these traits can apply to battered men too):

1. Has low self-esteem.
2. Believes all the myths about battering relationships.
3. Is a traditionalist about the home
4. Strongly believes in family unity and the prescribed feminine sex role stereotype.
5. Accepts responsibility for the batterer's actions.
6. Suffers from guilt yet denies the terror and anger she feels.
7. Presents a passive face to the world but has the strength to manipulate her environment enough to prevent further violence and possibly being killed.
8. Has a severe stress reaction with psycho-physiological complaints.
9. Uses sex as a way to establish intimacy.
10. Believes that no one will be able to help her resolve her predicament.

Clarke indicates that when counseling the battered, such characteristics must be kept in mind. When they are aware of abuse and the available resources, pastors can be prepared to offer leadership and counsel to battered persons in the churches. We can educate the church as a whole to reach out and help. We can give direct help to the battered person by encouraging support groups, giving referrals to adequate professionals, and through personal counseling.

The church is a community of caring, sharing, reconciling, and honoring. Its theology must challenge every attitude, belief, institution, and ideology that seeks to put down or belittles any member of society based on sex, sexual orientation, religion, or ethnicity. The focus of this chapter has been to examine and reveal the evils and myths surrounding abuse. It is hoped that as men and husbands we will be encouraged to work diligently to eradicate abuse from among us, whether we are guilty of it or not, so the love that God commands can flow uninhibitedly. Loving husbands and wives must stand with the victims and send a loud and clear message to the batters to stop and seek help.

We cannot afford to be silent bystanders. To be quiet is to play into the batterer's hands. As loving Christians, we are called upon to lead in this crusade to restore *agape* love to the battered and to speak out against this evil. We are called upon to provide resources and help to break the abuser self-destructives ways.

Our children, male and female, are looking for a brighter tomorrow. If we remain silent and do not address this bullying and stem this disease, there will be more failed marriages and create more challenge for our young adults when they get married.

Putting You Down

If you are in a relationship and you are thinking about making a decision to marry; you are going in with the understanding, belief and faith that you love this person, and that the persons loves you in return. However, it is important to keep an eye open that if there are any signs that your partner needs help to better show healthy loving actions, that you both address it. One of the most common ways in which one partner may bully the other is by putting him or her down. Emotionally attacking another person makes them more vulnerable and is often done to make the bully feel better. Whoever you are courting should always make you feel valuable and special. But, if you are not feeling valuable and special the truth is, he or she does not see it too, so they cannot make you feel it.

For the five years that Rev. Robinson knew Dalton, he had never turned down an opportunity to preach. This was the third youth Sunday that he had turned down the request to preach. After praying about it he decided to talk to Dalton about it. He felt that something was wrong because Dalton only started turning down the assignments since he got engaged to Georgette.

Apparently, Georgette had told Dalton not to embarrass her by going up to preach because he was not speaking proper English. They discussed the matter and prayed about it and Dalton confided in him how difficult it was for him not to preach because he felt it was his gift.

Why was Georgette putting Dalton down?
Should he give up preaching to please his future wife?

Manipulative Behavior

If you are in a relationship where your partner is a bully by using manipulative behaviors to get his/her way, draw the break on the relationship. This behavior is a love buster. That individual is only interested in a relationship where winning and being in the right brings happiness. Your relationship will not get better after marriage; it tends to get worse. Christian Marriage is a partnership. If you are experiencing a bullying partner now, that individual wants ultimate control and it will continue in marriage if it is not addressed before marriage. Ultimate control in the marriage must be God and God alone.

Here are a few manipulation devices that you need to be aware of and be prepared to deal with as you create and build a relationship that will glorify God and make society better:

1. The Silent Treatment
2. Temper-Tantrums
3. Name Calling
4. Guilt Trips
5. Passive-Aggressive Behavior

There are many different types of bullying within a relationship and it can be difficult to assess if one is a victim of bullying. If you suspect or feel like your partner may be bullying you, here are few questions you can ask yourself to make that determination. Are you feeling isolated from friends, family, church community or rejected by the one who claims he/she loves you most? Do you constantly feel threatened? If you answer YES to any of these questions, then more than likely you are in a relationship with a bully.

If you are in a relationship where you are experiencing any kind of bullying, then the first thing you need to know is that God is not in that behavior. Stand up for yourself and for the integrity of your Christian belief. If you truly love your future spouse, consider asking him/her to go to counseling with you to save the relationship.

Bullying will not stop on its own. Some young adults never stop their bullying behavior and carry it over into the marriage. Once you know how to recognize the signs, you can take the right steps to put a stop to the behavior, even if it means moving on from that relationship until God brings you the right person. You deserve to be treated better. An ounce of prevention is better than a pound of cure.

It is important that you get away from an abusive situation, but you need to do it in a safe way. Plan your escape well and let friends help you. Once you are out, allow someone to be with you all the time. Many people return to their abusive partners because they are lonely or feel that if they leave their partner, they will always be alone.

That is just what the abusive partner wants you to believe. But it is a lie. There is a wonderful life awaiting you, one where you can live without fear, live without pain and learn to love yourself and fulfill your life's goals. You deserve to feel free and fulfilled as a single young adult in a relationship that empowers you.

Discussion

1. What is the main reason someone becomes an abuser or bully?
2. What are the three steps of the abusive cycle?
3. How should you deal with feelings of being bullied?
4. What are the six types of love busters that Dr. Willard outlined?
5. How should you deal with the signs of abuse or bullying in your relationship?

Chapter 9

Premarital Discussions

Too often there is more emphasis on the wedding day itself but not enough on the formal premarital discussions. A trained pre-marriage and marriage counselor will know the right questions to ask and how to ask them. Asking the right questions will allow the engaged couple to think seriously about what they are getting into. It will allow them to move past love infatuations, all the fairy tales and realize that marriage is serious sacred business with a permanent bond and that it takes the favor of God, great commitment and compromise.

Everything that could potentially harm a marriage should be discussed during premarital counseling. No stone should be left unturned; no matter how uncomfortable the counselor or the couple gets. Some questions are going to be hard to deal with; some topics are going to appear as if they do not belong in Christian counseling and Christian marriage but nonetheless, they must be discussed. This means that the person conducting the pre-marital discussions cannot be squeamish or easily intimidated.

Pre-marital counseling is very important because it can help to clear up any misconceptions related to marriage and love. Pre-marriage counseling should help you to sit more secured in your relationship.

S.I.T.

What is sit you may ask? Good premarital counseling is designed to provide couple with the pertinent requirement of sit. S.I.T is an acronym for: Skills, Information and Tools.

One of the major reasons for given for divorce is summarized as a lack SIT. Sit is very necessary for new couples to have, to help them navigate this new enterprise call the married life. Persons coming to marriage today tend to come from different backgrounds and were socialized differently so it is wise to iron out any kinks before saying "I DO." Individuals will bring many issues in the marriage that will require the loving care of the other partner to provide the healing touch as a master potter.

I, Daniel read an article entitled, "Millennials Are Causing the U.S. Divorce Rate to Plummet - They're waiting until all is secure before tying the knot." It reported that Americans under the age of 45 have found a novel way to rebel against their elders: They're staying married. According to*** the U.S. divorce rate dropped 18 percent from 2008 to 2016, according to an *analysis* by University of Maryland sociology professor Philip Cohen. He felt the divorce rate's decline isn't a reflection of a decline in marriages in general. But rather, there is a change in the marriage culture today, and with that change marriages have a greater chance of lasting better and longer compare to marriages ten years ago. What is the change? According to Susan Brown, a sociology professor at Bowling Green State University, "**The characteristics of young married couples** today signal a sustained decline [in divorce rates] in the coming years." *The credit for the decline is* that the married population is **getting older** and more **highly educated**," People with college degrees are now *more likely to get married than those who have no more than a high-school education.*

Hence, having a third party helps couples to stay focused, identify kinks to work on, so they can set important goals and make sensible, concrete plans for their future.

So, what should the Christian pre-marital counseling/discussions address and cover? Is it okay to not cover the topics that make the couple or counselor uncomfortable? Are counselors doing a disservice to these couples when the pre-marital discussions are mediocre? Without a shadow of a doubt, engaged couple is shortchanged if there is even an ounce of mediocrity during the premarital discussions. It is for this very reason why every pastor who chooses to do pre-marital counseling should seek to be trained so that they can provide the best service to engaged couples.

Engaged couples should be prepared to invest quality time for their Pre-marital discussions in order to adequately cover all relevant grounds. This should be clearly communicated to all members of the church parish so that there are no surprises. A balanced pre-marital counseling should address the following areas along with any other areas that are deemed necessary:

1. Genogram and family's histories
2. Gender Roles
3. The gift of Sex – *Infidelity "Emotional"* HIV Status/Other forms of STDs
4. Intimacy/Keeping the Fire Burning
5. Money (Savings, Investment, Tithing and Giving, Lending, Joint Vs Single Accounts Living arrangement House Purchase/Rent
6. Leaving and Cleaving Seriously (Parents, Relatives, Friends etc.)
7. Conflict Management/Differences/Deal breakers
8. Friendships/Opposite sex
9. Social Media/Entertainment

10. Spirituality/Discipleship/Church Attendance/Involvement
11. Commitment/Compromise
12. Children
13. Hygiene
14. Continued Education
15. Plans for the wedding – large/small/budget
16. Evaluation of Marriage/Marriage Checkup

This is not a complete list.

Paul grew up in a house where his father was the bread winner while his mother stayed at home. His father never lifted a finger around the house and did not even know how to boil an egg. All his meals were provided by his wife who also made sure that the house was spotless. Jackie always knew how Paul felt about this issue but never thought it would affect their marriage the way it did. From the first week of the marriage Paul insisted that he did not want Jackie to work outside the home even though she was a professional and loved what she did. Then when that did not work he refused to help her with any of the household chores even though he got home hours before she did. How can they move forward?

Some persons might wonder why we need to go through all these areas, but sometimes what might seem obvious may not be as obvious as we think. On the off chance that some persons are not aware, then it is best to include as many points as possible. Wherever it is possible to fall short, then it should be discussed thoroughly until all parties are clear.

Genogram and Family Histories

Couples getting married need some family information that is best discovered in a *genogram*. *Genogram* provides couples with a graphic representation of each other *family tree* that displays detailed data on relationships among individuals of the family. It goes beyond just a traditional *family tree*. Genogram can be used to help couples see hereditary patterns and psychological factors that has punctuated a family relationship. The genogram helps couples see generational and family issues that can either enhance their new marriage and family or may see issues that need to be corrected in order for a healthy marriage and family life to ensue.

Gender Roles

This subject has gotten many men in the dog house because of how they were socialized. Parents are partly to be blamed for the way many boys are reared to feel that some things should only be done by women. Since this can be a potential cause for arguments then this forum should be used to iron out any misconceptions that any of them may have. If the woman was brought up in a home where domestic duties were shared between male and female, then she might resent having to do all the "woman" duties in the home. The situation becomes critical when both parties work outside of the home. Failure to discuss this area can result in a very unhappy, overworked wife and this is bad for a companionship marriage.

Sex

Every aspect of sex and sexuality should be discussed. This is an area where many church folks get squeamish but as stated before the counsellor should be comfortable discussing all topics. If this is not the case, then it is best to refer the couple elsewhere so that they can get the best help. These days there are so many different angles to this area; one would be surprised at the things that some Christian men and women ask of their spouses. There should be frank discussions about the following topics and any other that the counsellor deems necessary:

- Foreplay
- Oral sex
- Anal sex
- Pornography
- Inviting other persons into the bedroom
- Sex and fasting
- Withholding sex
- Birth Control
- HIV/AIDS and other forms of STDs

This is not an exhaustive list but just an example of the kinds of things that need to be covered before the couple says I do. People come from different backgrounds and as such it should never be assumed that things will just fall into place. There are so many Christian men and women who are addicted to porn and this can seriously harm a marriage. Porn can cause spouses to have unrealistic sexual expectations and very often this leaves a partner feeling that they cannot measure up. Porn will belittle a spouse who will eventually shut down, so whoever in the relationship that is addicted needs to realize the seriousness of this. If you ask many persons, they will hasten to say they are not addicted, and they are able to stop whenever they want to. However, an addiction is an addiction, and failure to deal with this can result in a failed marriage or an unfulfilled one.

For the couple who is inexperienced the counselor should provide a list of resources to assist and this should include books and videos. If the couple can afford it, then a referral to someone who specializes in this sort of thing should be made. For those persons who cannot afford it then other arrangements can be made for them to speak to a mature couple in the church if necessary.

In 1 Corinthians 7:5 the bibles states *"So don't refuse sex to each other, unless you agree not to have sex for a little while, in order to spend time in prayer. Then Satan won't be able to tempt you because of your lack of self-control"*. The operative word is "agree" therefore both parties must understand that if there is going to be any abstinence then it must be something that is discussed and agreed upon. Understanding the consequences of withholding sex from each other without a valid reason is very important for the prospective husband and wife. Understanding also what the word of God says about it is also paramount.

Charmaine was a 35 year old virgin when she got married to Reverend Butler. She never thought in a million years that she should ask him about his status because after all they both grew up in the church. When she got pregnant 6 months after the wedding she was on top of the world until she went to her first pre-natal clinic and she was tested for HIV. She was all too happy to do it because what could possibly go wrong? She can still remember the day the nurse told her she was HIV positive and her husband's confession and apology before he died. Fortunately they were able to protect her unborn child so she was free of the disease. How can Charmaine learn to trust again?

It is very difficult to recover from infidelity in a marriage so all precautions must be taken to guard against this. For some persons infidelity is a deal breaker and there is no discussion when this occurs. Even when a marriage recovers from infidelity, it is never quite the same because trust is broken. Taking time to discuss the effects of infidelity on a marriage is sensible as well as discussing the things that can lead to infidelity. The bible states in Ephesians 4:27 that we should not give the devil a foothold; therefore, every precaution must be taken to guard the marriage against infidelity because sometimes it just takes one small lapse in judgment. Couples need to bear in mind that there are different forms of infidelity and sometimes even though the actual deed is not done, a spouse can be severely hurt by emotional infidelity. In many ways emotional infidelity can be harder to break and more detrimental to a marriage.

HIV/AIDS Status and Other Forms of STDs

Many Christians have turned up their noses when this topic is to be discussed but HIV/AIDS and other forms of STDs is no joke. Certainly, there is cure for most, but to date there is no cure for HIV/AIDS so the wise person will take heed. Sometimes people forget that there is life before Christianity and that means persons may have been careless with their sexual health. For a level playing field all parties should know their status before entering into any marriage. The counselor can suggest that the test be done twice - 3 months apart; and that both parties share the result. There are lots of stories of Christian men and women who have contracted STDs from their very Christian partners so this is a must for the couple who is serious about pre-marital counseling.

Nobody should be offended by this request because it is quite reasonable given the times that we are living in. People might argue that if a person is a virgin then they do not have to do the test but since only God and that person knows this as a fact, then all persons must get tested. Further there are reported cases of people who were virgins who contacted HIV/STD. In the days and culture in which we are living there are many Christians who are still virgins, but they have participated in questionable sexual activities that can make them exposed to HIV/STD.

Marcia was dragging her feet in the kitchen again in the hopes that Doug would fall asleep before she got to bed. For the past couple of months Doug had been going to bed without taking a shower or brushing his teeth and she had a hard time being intimate with him. She was never good at speaking her mind and was afraid to hurt his feelings so instead she just made excuse after excuse. She had been praying about it and asked God for the right moment to talk to him about this and also the right way to say what she had to say. She got her opportunity that night because despite her best efforts Doug was very much awake so she took a deep breath and just told him the truth. Should she have spoken up earlier?

Intimacy/Keeping the Fire Burning

Many married couples fall into a rut in their romantic relationship after a few years of marriage and that can have disastrous consequences. Getting married does not mean the things we did to secure the marriage is over and that each party can throw down arms and relax. It means the full romantic race has just begun and each person has work to do; especially when their natural love drug begins to subside and after children come along. Sometimes women can be so taken up with the kids that they neglect their husbands. Talk about this in terms of how it can be avoided and provide simple practical ways to keep the fire burning. It does not have to be anything elaborate; it can be as simple as setting aside one night out of the month for a date night. If it is possible to do it more often than monthly, then that should be encouraged. Invite the couple to come up with simple things that they can do to not lose sight of each other. Encourage them also to document these things so they can have a point of reference when the time comes. The average couple does not set out to fall into this rut but sadly this happens. Being very conscious of this will help to stymie any deterioration and help the couple to grow closer as the years go by instead of drifting apart. Couples must always be reminded that marriage takes work and that it is not all peaches and cream.

> Jeffrey was very sensible where money was concerned. From the day he started working he has been saving and tithing. He was a very faithful tither and a great steward of his money. Megan was the exact opposite. She was up to her neck in debt and there was not a pair of heels that were not calling her name. She tithed whenever she had extra money and was very irresponsible with her money. Of course Jeffrey did not find this out until they got married and she was not able to contribute towards saving for the down payment on their first home. She was so much in debt that much of her money was going towards servicing the debts. Where do they go from here?

Money

Money can be a sore point that can throw cold water over any marriage. There is a reason why the Bible talks about money or things related to money in over 2,350 verses. The stress of finances can bring a marriage to its knees, so it is important to talk about things like savings, investment, tithing and giving, joint versus single accounts, lending to friends and relatives etc. If one half of the couple is a spendthrift and the other is a penny pincher as simple as this sounds it can wreak havoc. Now to be fair, neither the spendthrift nor the penny pincher is nice to love with so striking a balance is essential. A lot of how people deal with or think about money has to do with how they were brought up. Knowing where each other is coming from and understanding why the other thinks the way they do, can lighten the load. While on the subject of money, it might be a good idea to touch on the issue of salaries. Some men are not happy if the wife is earning more than the husband, but this is the reality sometimes. How will they deal with this should this happen? Is it a deal breaker for the husband/wife? How should the wife deal with it if she is actually earning more than her husband? What happens if one party should lose their job? All of these things should be discussed in detail until both parties are comfortable with whatever the issues are.

As a Christian couple tithing should be important to both parties. However, not everyone feels that this is necessary; one party might want to tithe after all bills are paid and the other might want to take the tithe out before anything else is done. Again, their views might be clouded by the way they were socialized so talking openly about this should clear the air before the fights begin. Being prepared takes the sting out of whatever the burning issue is at the moment.

The counselor can discuss certain principles that relate to savings and investment such as the 10-10-80 principle. Ten percent to tithing, ten percent to savings and live off the other 80%; this is not to say that the couple cannot save more than the ten percent but certainly a minimum of ten percent. The couple should be encouraged to save something, no matter how small it might seem. For this area it is quite okay to bring in a financial expert to discuss the couple's financial future if necessary. When is the right time to start investing or to get insurance? Who should be responsible for making sure all of this is done and payments are kept up to date? Should any one person be responsible? At the end of the day, whatever the decision is, each party must be on board and feel comfortable with it. Anything less will breed resentment, which can again lead to a breakdown in the marriage.

Another sore point can be the issue of lending to friends and relatives. Who is it okay to lend to and where should the funds to lend come from? How will they deal with lending should this topic come up? Should this be a joint discussion before lending to anyone? Or should this be an individual thing without including the other party? Couples should be encouraged to really think this through and give honest feedback so that there are no surprises during the marriage. Couples should try to come to a reasonable decision on this and stick to it.

Should the couple keep separate accounts or pool everything? Will there be separate accounts but a joint account for household bills? How much access should each have should they decide to keep separate accounts? Many women are taught to always have something put aside but how does the future spouse respond to something of this nature? Is he uncomfortable with this? Should there even be any discussion about individual accounts that were open perhaps before the couple met? Whatever makes both parties comfortable is what the couple should go with. There is no point in trying to push anything else on this couple; the final outcome must be decided by both parties with assistance from the counselor where necessary.

House Purchase/Rent

Where will the couple live after the grand day? Along with all the other preparations, this should be right up there with the selection of the ring and venue. It is a good idea for the couple to decide together on this for obvious reasons. If the first dwelling will be a rental, then there should be discussion about how long before purchasing a house. A good suggestion might be for the couple to register at a building society or some other financial institution where they can set up an account for persons to make donations in lieu of wedding gifts. That can be used towards down payment for the first home together.

> Earl was never a great communicator so when he and his wife has their first big fight, he completely shut down. His wife Maxine on the other hand came from a large family where there were hardly any secrets. She wanted to talk and he did not so she decided to move back in with her parents and share intimate details of their life with the entire family. This just made matters worse and Earl was at the point of divorce because he just did not understand why she had to leave and why she had to discuss this with her family. How best can they deal with this situation?

Leaving and Cleaving

Sometimes for a young couple leaving and cleaving can be very hard; especially for the woman who is very close to her parents. It is also very difficult for some parents, family members and friends to allow couples the opportunity to leave and cleave. Leaving and Cleaving is not an attempt to get the couple to cut off parents, family and friends but an attempt at keeping them focused on the fact that after the wedding day their number one priority is each other; not parents, relatives or friends. The counsellor should remind them of the importance of not sharing everything with friends and relatives. Instead taking the time to discuss issues with each other and finding a solution together before taking this outside of the house; unless this is absolutely necessary.

As two people from different backgrounds sharing a common space, there is bound to be disagreements, but the first line of defense should not be to run to parents or friends. It is imperative that the couple understand this. This is not going to be easy especially for a young couple but absolutely necessary because too many opinions can lead to a breakdown and this a very dangerous game to practice.

Conflict Management

Not knowing how to deal with conflicts can add fire to fury in any marriage. Whatever needs to be done to assist the couple even before the conflicts arise should definitely be done. Conflicts are going to arise because as stated before people come from different backgrounds. How the couple deal with the conflicts when they are faced with them will determine the quality of the marriage. At no point should the couple be led to feel as if there will be no conflicts; it should be made abundantly clear that conflicts are going to arise, so it is best to be prepared to deal with them as they come.

People have different ways to deal with conflict and some of these may not be healthy. A good rule of thumb would be to encourage the couple to deal with each conflict separately and once it has been settled to leave it there. Dealing with one issue at a time; or dealing with the issues as they arise will minimize animosity and discontentment. When conflicts come, the first line of defense should never be to run back home to parents or move out of the bedroom into another room or on to the couch. Some might even resort to sleeping head to toe but even that should be advised against. Couples must learn to talk things through objectively and pray over the situation so that they can reach the best conclusion; one that will honor God and the marriage. Finally, counselor should teach engaged couples' different types of conflict resolution methods to help them deal with the differences that life will bring to the marriage union. Conflict is rooted in differences!

Differences/Deal Breakers

The saying that "men are from mars and women are from Jupiter" is very fitting because men and woman are so different but yet they can complement each other if they know how to embrace their differences. The man who expects a woman to think like he does and the woman who expects a man to think like she does is not ready for marriage. Many couples run into problems because men are expecting women to think like men and women are expecting men to think like women. As long as the couple understands that it is okay to think differently, then half the battle has been won. Couples who have learnt how to embrace their differences, even during courtship, will have less conflicts and a more rewarding relationship. What is the deal breaker for each person in the relationship? What is the one thing (if any) that would cause the

individual to end the marriage without question? It is important that couples do not hide deal breakers from each other. Discussing this frankly will let the other person know which end is up. That is the reason why the premarital counseling must be no holds barred. This is the time to air all grouses and iron out the kinks before the journey starts. Persons will be tempted to hide deal breakers because they do not want to seem unfair or fussy but if this is something that will cause an individual to walk out of the marriage then it needs to be wide open on the table.

Janice and Bryan had been best friends and neighbors since they were in kindergarten. Unknown to Janice, Bryan had been in love with her since high school but always felt he had time to tell her. Now she was married and the feelings were still there and it was hard to listen to her talk about her new husband. Now they were having marital problems and looked forward to the times when she would cry on his shoulder and complain about her husband. One day things got out of hand and they ended up kissing. Janice now realized that it might not be such a good idea after all to have an opposite sex best friend, especially one who was obviously in love with her. Should she tell her husband about the kiss and how will she deal with her best friend of so many years?

Opposite Sex Friendships

How does the couple feel about having an opposite sex best friend? Is it appropriate for a married couple to have opposite sex best friends? Is it wise? There are many opinions about this, but it is the couple who must decide what is best for their relationship. Of course, the counselor can offer an opinion on the matter considering that this can turn into a fiasco very quickly without proper monitoring. It certainly is not wise to have an opposite sex best friend as a married person. There are too many things that can go wrong. If one person is not comfortable with this situation then definitely, out of respect, the friendship needs to be discontinued.

Megan has always been a social media darling. She had a huge following on Facebook, twitter and google. She referred to them as her fans that needed to hear from her all through the day. Roger still had a regular phone and he had no social media accounts. Before they got married he was annoyed by her attachment to technology but he felt this would change once they got married. However this was so far from the truth as Megan spent more time with her followers than she did with Roger posting things he considered private. She felt that her fans had a right to know what was going on with her but he was very frustrated. How can this couple work through these issues?

Social Media

Technology has many benefits but unfortunately if this is not used wisely in a marriage then one person can be left feeling lonely and frustrated. The advent of the smart phone has also dealt another serious blow to relationships. When a couple's cyber life is more important than their significant other then there is need for some serious intervention. For a young couple, this will need conscious effort because so many persons are attached to their phones these days. Whether the addiction is just one person or both, this can be detrimental to the marriage. Persons mean well but for a young man or woman who is so attached to their phone this might prove more difficult than one could possibly imagine. It might be wise to encourage the couple to start practicing before the wedding to power down at some point so that it is not so hard to do once they say "I DO"

Social media is a dangerous weapon if not used wisely. How does the couple deal with things like the very popular

Facebook? Almost everyone has an account and some persons are still not quite sure how to conduct themselves on this medium. Should you add your spouse as a friend? Should your spouse have access to your account/password? What is appropriate to post? How much time should be spent updating on a daily basis? All of these and more are important questions to seek to answer during the pre-marital counseling. It has become the norm these days to spend more time updating status than spending face time with others. No marriage can survive with this kind of attitude so much emphasis must be placed on this lopsided phenomenon.

What about email accounts? Should there be a joint email account, so each couple is fully aware of whatever is coming in? Should each person keep their personal emails but have a joint email account? Should there be full disclosure in terms of the passwords for personal emails? Marriages today face a myriad of problems that did not exist years ago so the adjustment for many young couples is much harder. The distractions brought on by technology are real so this should definitely be on the agenda. It cannot and should not be ignored!

Josh could not understand why Marie was out again at another club on Saturday night. He knew she liked going to clubs but why was she still out with her friends so late on Saturday nights when she had to be on the choir in the morning? Why was it more important for her to be out with her girlfriends leaving him alone at home almost every Saturday night? Marie could not understand why Josh was making such a big deal; after all she was just having fun with her friends. Josh did not even feel it was okay to go to the movies as a form of entertainment and he and Marie has had several arguments over what is considered appropriate entertainment for a Christian. How do they determine what is appropriate entertainment?

Entertainment

What constitutes entertainment for one half of the couple might not be the same for the other half. Some persons can spend the entire day sitting in front of the television and that is quite fine if you are a single person. This might not work as well for the person who is married. What if one person thinks it is a sin to go to the movies, but the other person loves going to the movies? Is it okay to go to the movies without the spouse who thinks it is a sin? The counselor has to steer the conversation in the right direction and talk through it. Does one person feel comfortable attending house parties and the other does not? What is considered appropriate entertainment for both persons? If one person loves to be at home and the other loves to socialize this can cause one spouse to feel abandoned. Some sort of compromise will be necessary here because forcing the person who does not like to socialize into this situation often might lead to resentment. The counselor has to help the couple understand and appreciate their differences so they can they can coexist amicably.

Maxine got pregnant at 15 and had a daughter who lived with her mum. Her church family did not know about this and neither did Brad, her fiancé. Each day it got harder and harder to tell him her secret and as the wedding day drew closer and closer she felt as if she was going to stop breathing. How would he react if he found out that she has a 14 year old daughter? In his conversations he always said he was not marrying any woman who had kids so she had to find a way to tell this to him before the wedding. How could she break this to him without losing the love of her life?

Children

Kids must be discussed as early as possible in the relationship and most certainly if there is a marriage proposal. If the man or woman had children prior to the marriage, then this should never be a secret – even if the kids are living elsewhere. Some men do not want to marry a woman who has had kids and some women feel the same way about men who have had kids before. The worst time to find this out is after the marriage so there must be full disclosure, as uncomfortable as this might be especially for the woman.

This might seem quite trivial and obvious, but it can cause serious problems down the road. If one party wants to have many children and the other can only see one child in their future, this is a recipe for disaster. Now this is not about a spouse who is not quite sure, this is about a spouse who is adamant and unbending where this is concerned. This is a big red flag that should not be ignored. Here it is very important that the persons be brutally honest because the only sure birth control is abstinence. If any spouse is adamant that they only want a specific amount of kids any deviation from this rule can lead to serious complications and many marriages might not be able to survive that. The issue of kids can be a tricky subject; whether future or kids from a previous relationship. It is expected that by this time there would have been full disclosure where all current kids are concerned. There have been cases where women had abortions when they were younger and due to complications from this abortion, they are not able to get pregnant. In the case where this is known then the future husband should know about this. Even if the woman does not feel comfortable discussing this in the counselling session, she should be aware that this conversation must take place with her future husband. During this section the counsellor should also touch on infertility; reminding the couple that this is not always a female problem. Anyone of the two can have a problem producing children so it is very important that everyone understands this. A man who thinks that this is only a female problem might need to be properly educated on the subject before continuing with the counselling. The discussion must cover ways for the couple to deal with this in case it happens because infertility can drive a wedge between the most loving couple.

Gracie was determined that her wedding would be bigger and better than her arch enemy, Judith. She knew that Marcus had just gotten a new job and that he had told her that they had to go easy on the spending. The need to brag and compete got the better of her however and she went way over budget without speaking to Marcus. When Marcus found out that she had maxed out the credit card he gave her to pay for the things they had agreed on, he threatened to call off the wedding. After much intervention and her returning the unnecessary items, the crisis was averted. How should Gracie deal with this unhealthy competition she has with Judith?

Plans for the Wedding

This not so obvious area must not be forgotten. Planning a wedding can be stressful and sometimes women tend to overspend without regard for the gentleman. No matter how much a bride to be wants to splurge, care must be taken to keep the spending at a reasonable level so that the man does not feel overwhelmed. A lot of men will not openly say it is too much but how much is to be spent should be a joint decision and nothing should be done until the couple comes to a reasonable understanding. Talking about this with a third party can help a great deal.

Spirituality/Discipleship/Church Attendance/Involvement

> Before the marriage, Lillian was at church every night. Arthur attended church on a regular basis but kept it to Sundays, Wednesdays and the once per month men's meeting. He was quite aware that Lillian spent a lot of time at church but he did not see the need for them to discuss this before the wedding. He just thought that as a married woman she would adjust the times she spent at church. How wrong he was about that. After the marriage Lillian did not think it was necessary to adjust the times she spent at church. Many times she went straight from work to church. She felt that Arthur wanted her to fall back on her responsibilities at church and she did not want anyone to think that she had changed because she got married. How can they resolve this?

As hard as this may seem, time should be spent talking about this. Some persons are heavily involved in church; sometimes they can be at church almost every night for one meeting or the other. For a single person this is fine, but this might not be such a good idea for a person who is married. Couples need to figure out together which days they are going to dedicate to attending meetings at church. Some amount of compromise has to take place for the strengthening of the marriage.

Barbara was very serious about her education and had her plans for each step of the way. Right now she was ready to do her Masters degree in Education and she was already registered for classes that start in one month. The problem is she had not said anything to her new husband Kevin. She did not see the need to discuss any of this with him. Kevin only had a high school diploma and was not interested in going beyond that. He was more interested in providing for his family and the small business he ran did that very well. Should Barbara have discussed this with Kevin before she made such a decision?

Continued Education

Many times, women are more interested in higher education than men. If there is a chance that one party is considering higher education during the course of the marriage, then this should be talked about. Attending any kind of school during a marriage will need adjustments and compromise on every member of that household. Depending on the work load it can seriously impact a lot of things so great care must be taken to keep the marriage intact. The prospective wife or husband must be made aware of what they are in for.

Casy was excited about the marriage seminar that was announced at church. She thought this could be something that she and her new husband could attend on an annual basis as a means of evaluating their marriage and keep things in check. However Marvin would not hear of it. He does not see why they need to attend these things because people might think their marriage is in trouble. Casy believes that this is a great way to keep their marriage viable and out of trouble. Is Casy on the right track or should she listen to Marvin and wait until there is trouble before seeking help?

Evaluation of Marriage/Marriage Checkup

A couple should never wait until there is trouble but should evaluate their marriage as often as possible. A good way to do this is to attend seminars where they can learn about ways to keep the marriage viable.

Chapter 10

The Forever Love

Byron sighed when he saw that his mother was calling him again. He knew why she was calling and he did not have the energy to deal with that right now.

She had been at him to get a prenuptial agreement before he got married to Melissa.

Byron admits he had done well for himself but how could he tell Melissa that he wanted to protect himself in case the marriage did not work out? He was in this for the long haul and he believed that she was too. A prenuptial agreement was the furthest thing from his mind.

He believed that discussing any such agreement is disrespectful to his future wife and he needed to find a way to get this across to his mum.

Should Byron listen to his mother and discuss this with Melissa or should he just do what he knows is best?

What is the best thing to do in this case?

Forever love is trans-generational! It is a love that carries on long after you are gone from this world. Many wonderful gifts, benefits and blessings can be passed from generation to generation, but the greatest gift a father and mother can give their children is a healthy loving community; a community where children will learn the appropriate ways to communicate in a loving way.

Love language is that emotional vehicle through which one feels and experiences love. When husbands and wives find each other's love language and use that language to communicate with each other then children learn from this. This will in turn form a wonderful foundation for their children's lives. According to Chapman, "Children who feel loved by their parents and peers will develop a primary emotional love language based on their unique psychological makeup and the way their parents and other significant persons expressed love to them. Children who do not feel loved by their parents and peers will also develop a primary love language" (14).

Chapman modified these two descriptions by saying, "Poor programming does not mean they cannot become good communicators. But it does mean they will have to work at it more diligently than those who had a more positive model" (14).

George Barna, president of the Barna Research Group, noted on his web site that the impact of such widespread divorce has left its mark on young people. "One of the most striking findings in our recent survey among teenagers is that when we asked them to name their top goals for the future, one of the highest rated was to get married and have the same spouse for life." This is the hope of our young people. They want a forever love.

Barna says, "That's a remarkable goal—one that reflects their own exposure to, and rejection of, a family that has to survive divorce, for whatever reasons. Since millions of those teens have never had a healthy marriage modeled for them, we can only pray that they will have the strength of character and the support systems available to make their goal a reality."

Many children do not have a realistic view of marriage. They have flawed models around them, and they are waiting for someone to show them the way.

Different family traits determine the emotional growth of children. However, a husband's love for his wife is one of the greatest ingredients necessary for emotional health and maturity. Loving husbands and wives live their lives knowing that the love they have, and practice is not only meant for them, but that it must continue through their children. When husbands fulfill the command to love their wives, they are modeling an attitude and behavior that will provide a solid foundation for their children's future happiness. Raising emotionally stable children is only possible in a loving environment. Young adults who lived in homes where there was a loving relationship between their parents will, more than likely, provide a loving environment for their children.

Society expects children to demonstrate love to their mothers and fathers—usually through obedience. However, I do observe that children find it easier to love and obey their parents when they see their parents demonstrate love to each other. In my opinion, the greatest gift a husband will ever give to his children is to love their mother.

One of the biggest problems in our society today is that most homes are starving for love. Some women are changeable and moody; men sometimes get confused and find it difficult to display love to their wives. When they realize this is happening, husbands must put concentrated effort into their marriages and choose to demonstrate agape love because this will help their children's future relationships.

It is commonly believed that men work from a logical point of view while women work from an emotional point of view. A husband may give his wife a rose today to demonstrate his love for her, but if he tries the same thing the next day it may not be accepted. The husband may not understand why she is not receptive the second time. It is important to note that God did not command husbands to understand their wives, but He did command husbands to love them. When husbands shower their wives with love, with the help of God, they will be able to meet their every need and build a healthier environment for their children. A properly loved wife and mother is a happy person, which in turn produces a happy and loving home with well-adjusted children.

Today, because of the love-starved homes that many of our children are living in, it is very difficult for them to make that love connection when they become adults. The homes that should be havens of rest are filled with many selfish and abusive parents. Hence, many of our children do not have a point of reference for loving another human being.

If a child lives with love, he will learn to accept himself for who he is. Many children are living in fear of divorce because their parents do not show love to each other. When love is missing between a husband and a wife, in due time, separation or divorce becomes a reality. Trust in God, along with love, is the only thing that can truly glue a family together. Love is the central nervous system of every family and should be the ultimate goal in obtaining a healthy, sturdy, and happy family.

Let me pause here to directly caution women. Before you enter into a relationship, be sure the man loves you as a whole person. Be sure he loves you for yourself; not for your possessions or your outward beauty. All those things will change with time. Marriage will not change who you are; instead, it will enhance or complete you. If the husband enters the relationship with the right attitude, respect, commitment and knowledge, then love will only get better with time and anything else will wane. First Corinthians 13:13 says, "And now these three remain: faith, hope and love. But the greatest of these is love" (*NIV*). This verse is referring to spiritual things such as tongues, knowledge, and prophesying which will pass away, "but faith, hope and love will never pass away."

Everything in marriage will change, but love is the only constant. King Solomon tells us in his commentaries on love that not even the grave can conquer it. Love will follow us to our graves, and it will continue in the hearts of our spouses and children. Therefore, for this reason, it behooves us to continue giving love because it will last through eternity.

Loving Forever

"I will love you forever" is probably the oldest expression ever used between lovers. This statement was, and still is, like music to the ears of those who receive it. However, today one wonders at the meaning of these words. The question that should be asked in response to this statement is, How long is forever? Is it until the "in-love" nostalgic feeling dies? Is it until we grow apart? Or is it until we find some irreconcilable differences?

These words, *I will love you forever*, are a vow to the receiver and a conscious choice made as part of a Christian marriage vow. "I will forsake all others . . . and I will love you forever, until death do us part." You may have thought that these words were made just as part of a contract; however, these words were registered in heaven in a covenant witnessed by God according to Malachi's description of the marriage of Israel. "You asked, '*Why?*' It is because the Lord is acting as the witness between you and the wife of your youth, because you have broken faith with her, though she is your partner, the wife of your marriage covenant" (2:14, *NIV*). God is expecting husbands and wives to honor their marriage covenant to love each other forever.

A man usually remembers when he fell in love. He met someone whose physical characteristics and personality traits created enough electrical shock to trigger his "love-alert" system. The bells went off and he set into motion the process of getting to know the woman and then they get married. A few months or years later the euphoric feelings have waned, and they say that the "love tank" is empty, thus the initial attraction is not as potent as it once was. Many people enter their marriage union with the euphoric experience of falling in love. In his book, *The Five Love Languages*, Dr. Gary Chapman mentions that Dorothy Tennov, a psychologist who has done long-range study on the "in-love" phenomenon, indicates that the average life span of a romantic obsession is two years. When love wanes, many couples ask what happens to that "in-love" feeling? Was it real? Yes, those feelings were real, but the problem is those feelings were coupled with faulty information that euphoria would last forever.

Others consider falling in love to be unreal. One such person is Dr. M. Scott Peck. He gives three reasons why the falling-in-love feelings are not real. Falling in love is not an act of the will or a conscious choice; it is not real because it is effortless. The one who is in love is not genuinely interested in fostering the personal growth of the other person.

However, there are countless testimonies of marriages that started with individuals falling in love and today they are still happily married; so, it must be real. There are many couples that started with the in-love feeling, and they never stopped to think through the reason why their "love tanks" are empty. They continue to live in their misery or they divorce. Neither of these choices is the answer. Love is a choice; and if a couple makes a commitment to love forever there must be another alternative to pursue real love. Dr. Chapman said, "Our most basic need is not to fall in love but to be genuinely loved by another, to know a love that grows out of reason and choice, not instinct. . . . That kind of love requires effort and discipline. One of the main reasons for ineffective love communication is that there is seldom the same love language communicated between husbands and wives" (33).

The Christian marriage is not merely a contract between two persons. It is a covenant that can only be nullified by death or by God. Therefore, when a couple enters into a Christian marriage and makes a vow to love forever, God holds them answerable to their contractual obligations. The problem in many marriages is the lack of healthy and full "love tanks." In his book titled *The Five Love Languages*, Dr. Gary Chapman stated that there are five emotional love languages that people speak and understand. However, there are unlimited ways to express love within a love language. The important thing is to be able to communicate the love language of your spouse. If husbands and wives would learn to speak each other's love language, then they would see an increase in their "love tanks" and a decline in the divorce rate.

Because it is so easy to get a divorce, many people use it as a way out of their marriage rather than trying to repair what is wrong. Many people do not believe it is too easy to get a divorce. Instead, it is too easy to get married. All one needs is $20 and a blood test. Those who perform marriages are given permission to marry anyone who wants to be married. After marriage, newlyweds seem to think that once you get into your first fight, the marriage is not going to work, and the perfect person is waiting for them in their next marriage. There is no attitude of "sticking with it" and trying to work out the problems. Divorce is not the only choice. There is a better way; marriage is until death.

Some denominations are encouraging all clergy to marry only those couples that first take a marriage preparation course; that is a good beginning. However, I do think that just as people are required by law to study the "Driver's Handbook" and practice their driving skills before they are granted a license to drive, a similar requirement should be in place for persons who want to get married.

Many churches are spearheading initiatives to promote marriage preparation. Couples are encouraged to accept mediation before considering divorce, and there are courses in public schools that deal with values and relationships. Legislation will help to decrease the divorce rate, but the true answer to divorce is a rekindled love relationship.

Seven Keys to Forever love

The late Dr. Horace Wards, senior pastor of South Cleveland Church of God, in Cleveland, Tennessee, presented another way that husbands can build their love lives when he addressed his local church's Lay Ministry breakfast. He said, "There are seven key ingredients to restore and maintain a great love life or to keep the sparkle in your love life." They are:

1. Commitment
2. Companionship
3. Considerateness
4. Care
5. Communication
6. Compassion
7. Consummation

After listening to this address, I reflected on what I mentioned in Chapter 1 about the five different types of love. I realized that the above list, when properly applied, would supply all the different types of love. *Agape* love is unconditional love and such love requires commitment in order for it to truly function. *Eros* love, which is romantic love, requires considerateness in providing the romantic needs of each mate. *Phileo* love is expressed through friendship and it takes genuine companionship to provide a good friendship. *Storge* love is expressed in the feeling of belonging and requires care when reaching out to meet such needs. Finally, *epithumia* love, which is lovemaking, is the physical way God designed for husbands and wives to consummate their love.

In the areas Dr. Ward listed, there must be a passion to communicate clearly and concisely in each type of love so that marriage will grow and become sweeter with each passing day.

Love will either grow healthy or unhealthy depending on how husbands and wives relate to it in their relationship. If husbands apply Dr. Ward's formula, guided by the indwelling presence of the Holy Spirit, love will grow. The apostle Paul charged husbands to love their wives and charged wives to submit to their husbands. He charged them both to be completely filled and to be continuously filled with the Spirit of God rather than being filled with the spirit that leads to debauchery (Ephesians 5:18). A person who is Spirit-filled will express love for his or her spouse. The Holy Spirit will teach that individual how to love.

One of the problems we face today is that many of our believers are filled with the wrong spirit. Many of our churches in North America seem to be filled with the spirit of the world where marriage is concerned. When the Holy Spirit controls our spirits, we will love our spouses the way God intended. However, when other spirits influence our spirits, we will not have the necessary power to handle the difficulties and stresses of marital relationships, and ultimately, we will be tempted to neglect nurturing love.

When you get married, if your "love tank" seems to be running dry or your feeling of love for your spouse seems to be diminishing, there *is* hope if the Holy Spirit still resides in you. Love is a choice you make. Christ chose to love you and me even while we were still sinners. His love gave us life. The choice we make to love our spouse is unconditional: "I will love you forever."

The Forever Glue

The *only* power that can separate true love is a forever God. Jesus said, in Matthew 19:6, "Wherefore they are no more twain, but one flesh. What therefore God hath *joined* [italics mine] together, let not man put asunder."

The Greek word for *joined* is *proskollao* which means to join fast together—to glue together, to cement together; to be joined in the closest union possible, to be bound together; to be so totally united that two become one. Therefore, to join here means a spiritual union. It is a union higher and stronger than the union of parent and child. It is a union that means more than living together, more than having sex and bearing children. It is a spiritual fullness, a spiritual sharing of life together—dedication, consecration, completeness, satisfaction—that makes husbands and wives the exclusive possession of God and each other. God designed such a cleaving or spiritual union, and only God can dissolve the bond.

Three unions take place in a true marriage bond joined together by God. They are the physical union, the sharing of their bodies (1 Corinthians 7:2-5); the mental union, the sharing of their lives, hopes, and dreams, and the working together to realize those hopes and dreams; and, the spiritual union, the sharing, melting, and molding of their spirits (Ephesians. 5:25-33). These unions are designed to grow daily as they are watered in love.

Let us not forget that God is the author of love and He is the One who works the "joining." If He dwells in you, He will provide you with the necessary grace to live with situations that are sometimes unpleasant or will provide a way to overcome or solve the problems. There are many good books on the market that can help Christian marriages. If the Creator, the God of love, resides in you, He is willing to provide the necessary love you need to cause your marriage love bonds to grow and mature with time and age. If you will genuinely seek His help, you will receive it today.

God has never commanded; and would never command His children to do anything without giving the necessary tools or ingredient to fulfill His command. So, as you prepare to take on the task of loving your spouse forever, if you are in need of love healing and your world seems to be falling apart, let me encourage you to begin afresh by inviting the God of love to heal and restore your love so you can enter marriage committed to a forever love.

Discussion

1. How can parents demonstrate their love language to their children?
2. Why are so many families starving for love? How can that affect our children?
3. In what ways do husbands work from a logical point of view?
4. In what ways do women work from an emotional point of view?
5. When you tell your spouse "I will love you forever," what did the words really mean to you? Do they mean the same today?
   Why do you think so many young couples today do not take the marriage vows seriously?

Conclusion

Now that you have read this book and gained some new insights about your love responsibilities, communicate with your future husband or wife. Ask questions. Find out what his or her love language is. Develop a habit of practicing each other's love language, restore your love, grow in love and, if needed, seek qualified pastoral marital counseling to help you maintain your revived love. Above all else, pray! The God of love can bring you and your spouse together, and you will be able to say as John did in 1 John 4:11, "Beloved, if God so loved us, we ought to also love one another."

If you and your spouse have begun to use the suggestions mentioned in this book, I believe you are ready to rebuild and enrich your love relationship. My prayer is that, each day, you will turn to God for guidance in your marriage. He will teach you how to love, and He will guide you in that love, because He is love.

Ways to Enhance Romance

Here are some suggestions given by Steve and Mary Prokopchak in their book, *Called Together*, which you can use to improve your love life.

Ways a Husband Can Express Love to His Wife

Husbands need to evaluate the ways they express their love to their wives every day. Listed below are some ways to demonstrate your love. Go over this list and circle the ways you may be neglecting to show love for your wife. Ask your wife to go over the list and put a check mark in front of the ways she would like for you to express love. Ask her to add other ways to the list. Here are some ways to demonstrate your love.

1. Function as the loving leader of your home.
2. Frequently tell her you love her.
3. If she does not work outside the home, give her an agreed-upon amount of money to spend in any way she chooses.
4. Lead family devotions regularly.
5. Do something spontaneous and zany—don't always be predictable.
6. Share the household chores.
7. Take care of the children for at least three hours every week so she has free time to do whatever she wants.
8. Take her out for dinner or do some fun thing at least once a week.
9. Do the "fix-it" jobs she wants done around the house.
10. Greet her when you come home with a smile, a hug, a kiss and an "I am glad to see you. I really missed you today."
11. Give her a lingering kiss.

12. Pat her on the shoulder, hold her hand, and caress her frequently.
13. Be willing to talk to her about her concerns and don't belittle her for having them
14. Look at her with an adoring expression.
15. Sit close to her.
16. Rub her back.
17. Shave, take a bath and brush your teeth before you have sexual relations.
18. Wear her favorite aftershave lotion.
19. Write love notes or letters to her.
20. Let her know you appreciate her and what you appreciate about her. Do this often and for things that are sometimes taken for granted.
21. Fulfill her implied or unspoken wishes as well as the specific requests she makes of you.
22. Anticipate what she might like and surprise her by doing it before she asks.
23. Play together, share her hobbies and recreational preferences enthusiastically and include her in yours.
24. Set a good example before the children.
25. Talk about her favorably to the children when she can hear you, and even when she cannot.
26. Brag about her good points to others; let her know you are proud to have her as your wife.
27. Maintain your own spiritual life through Bible study, prayer, regular church attendance and fellowship with God's people.
28. Structure your time and use it wisely; be on time to go places.
29. Make plans prayerfully and carefully.
30. Ask her advice when you have problems or decisions to make.
31. Follow her advice unless to do so would violate Biblical principles.

32. Fulfill your responsibilities.
33. Be sober, but not somber, about life.
34. Have a realistic, Biblical, positive attitude toward life
35. Discuss plans with your wife before you make decisions, and when the plans are made, share them fully with your wife, giving reasons for making the decisions you did.
36. Thank her in creative ways for her attempts to please you.
37. Ask forgiveness often, and say, "I was wrong and will try to change."
38. Actually change areas of your life that you know need changing.
39. Share your insights and good experiences with her.
40. Plan a mini-honeymoon.
41. Give some expression of admiration when she wears a new dress or your favorite negligee.
42. Gently brush her leg under the table.
43. Be reasonably happy to go shopping with her.
44. Relate what happened at work or whatever you did apart from her.
45. Reminisce about the early days of your marriage.
46. Express appreciation for her parents and relatives.
47. Take her out to breakfast.
48. Agree with her about getting a new dress or some other item.
49. Thank her when she supports your decisions and cooperates.
50. Especially make it a matter of celebration when she supports and helps you when you know she does not fully agree.
51. Ask her to have sexual relations with you and seek to be especially solicitous of her desires.
52. Express gratitude when she tries to please you.
53. Buy gifts for her.

54. Remember anniversaries and other events that are special to her.
55. Watch the TV program she wants to watch or go where she wants to go instead of doing what you want to do. Do it cheerfully and enthusiastically.
56. Be cooperative and appreciative when she holds you, caresses or kisses you.
57. Be cooperative when she tries to arouse you and desires to have sexual relations. Never make fun of her for expressing her desires.
58. Run errands gladly.
59. Pamper her and make a fuss over her.
60. Be willing to see things from her point of view.
61. Be lovingly honest with her. Don't withhold truth that may hinder your present or future relationship.
62. Indicate you want to be alone with her and talk or just lie in each other's arms.
63. Refuse to cop out, blow up, attack, shift blame, withdraw or exaggerate when she seeks to make constructive suggestions or discuss problems.
64. Give her your undivided attention when she wants to talk.
65. Cheerfully stay up past your bedtime to solve problems or to share her burdens.
66. Get up in the middle of the night to take care of the children so she can continue to sleep.
67. Hold her close while expressing love when she is hurt, discouraged, weary, or burdened.
68. Plan vacations and trips with her.
69. Help her yourself instead of telling the children to "help mommy."
70. Be eager to share a good joke or some other interesting information you have learned.
71. Join with her in a team ministry in the church.
72. Do a Bible study or research project together?

73. Establish a family budget.
74. Keep yourself attractive and clean.
75. Be a cooperative, helpful host when you have people over for dinner or fellowship.
76. Ask her to pray with you about something.
77. Spend time with the children in play, study and communication.
78. Acknowledge that there are some specific areas or ways in which you need to improve.
79. Refuse to disagree with her in the presence of others.

Ways a Wife Can Express Love to Her Husband

Evaluate the way you express your love to your husband. Go over this list and circle any ways you may be neglecting to show love for your husband. Ask your husband to go over the list and put a check mark in front of the ways he would like you to express love. Ask him to add other things to the list.

1. Greet him at the door when he comes home with a smile, a hug, a kiss and an "Am I glad to see you! I really missed you today."
2. Have a cup of coffee or tea ready for him when he comes home from work or a trip.
3. Give him a lingering kiss.
4. Let him know you like being with him and make arrangements so you can spend time with him without giving the impression that you really should or would rather be doing something else.
5. Be willing to talk to him about his concerns without belittling him for having these concerns.
6. Support him and cooperate with him enthusiastically when he has made a decision.
7. Tease and flirt with him.

8. Seek to arouse him and sometimes be the aggressor in sexual relations.
9. Ask him to have sexual relations more than he would expect you to.
10. Express yourself passionately during sexual relations.
11. Caress him.
12. Look at him with an adoring expression.
13. Sit close to him.
14. Hold his hand.
15. Rub his back.
16. Wear his favorite nightgown or dress or perfume.
17. Express your love in words or notes.
18. Let him know you appreciate him and what you appreciate about him.
19. Do this often and for things that are sometimes taken for granted.
20. Frequently fulfill his unspoken wishes as well as the specific requests he makes of you. Try to anticipate what he might like and surprise him by doing it before he asks.
21. Play together (tennis, golf, party games, etc.).
22. Enthusiastically share with him in devotions and prayer; seek to set a good example for the children concerning their attitudes toward devotions and prayer.
23. Maintain your own spiritual life through Bible study and prayer.
24. Structure your time and use it wisely.
25. Be willing to face and solve problems even if it requires discomfort, change, and much effort.
26. Fulfill your responsibilities.
27. Ask him for his advice and frequently follow it.
28. Be ready to leave at the appointed time.
29. Stand with him and support him in his attempts to raise your children for God.

30. Thank him in creative ways for his attempts to please you.
31. Ask for forgiveness by saying, "I was wrong and will try to change."
32. Actually change areas of your life that you know need changing.
33. Work with him on his projects.
34. Read books or magazine articles he asks you to read and share your insights.
35. Let him know when he has to make decisions that you believe he will make the right choice and that you will wholeheartedly support him in whatever decision he makes, provided the decision does not violate clearly revealed Biblical principles.
36. Be his best cheerleader and fan.
37. Buy gifts for him.
38. Show, genuine interest in his hobbies.
39. Watch or attend sporting events with him.
40. Listen to him sing and play the guitar or piano.
41. Attend a class he teaches.
42. Keep the house neat and clean.
43. Cook creative and nutritious meals, or praise him when he does.
44. Have devotions with the children when he is not able to be there.
45. Maintain his disciplinary rules when he is not present.
46. Be cooperative and appreciative when he holds you, caresses you, or kisses you.
47. Lovingly give him your input when you think he is in error.
48. Offer constructive suggestions when you think he could improve or become more productive. Don't push or preach or do this in such a way that you belittle him, instead seek non-threatening ways to help him become the man God wants him to be.

49. Run errands gladly.
50. Seek to complete, not compete with him; be the best member on his team and seek to convince him that you are just that.
51. Be lovingly honest with him. Do not withhold the truth that may hinder your relationship or future trust and closeness.
52. Be willing to see things from his point of view; believe the best about what he does or says.
53. Pamper him and make a fuss over him.
54. Be happy and cheerful.
55. Refuse to nag.

There is a multiplicity of ways to express love to your spouse. Since people express and experience love in different ways, take time to share with each other how you can show love and develop a system that will help you to accomplish the suggestions on this list. Only you and your spouse know your true feelings—love languages—so talk about what will satisfy the love needs you both have and do your best to cultivate those needs.

Bibliography

Adams, Carol. J., *Creative Pastoral Care and Counseling Series: Women Battering*. Minneapolis: Fortress Press, 1994.

Allen, M.A. and I.M. Allen, *Basics of Qualitative Research: Techniques and Procedures for Developing Grounded Theory*, 2nd edition. Sage Publications, 1998.

Barclay, William, *The Daily Study Bible: New Testament*. Westminster: John Knox Press, 1993.

Barna, George, Barna Research Group. 21 Dec. 1999. Web

Blanchi, Eugene and Rosemary Ruether, *From Machismo to Mutuality: Essays on Sexism and WomanMan Liberation*. New York: Paulist Press.1993.

Bradbury, Thomas, *The Development Course of Marital Dysfunction*. Cambridge University Press, 1998.

Browne, Angela, *When Battered Women Kill*. New York: Free Press, 1987.

Carter, Steven, *The Love Laws*. NewYork: M Evans and Company Inc., 2001.

Chapman, Gary Ph.D., *The Five Love Languages*. Chicago: Northfield Publishing, 1995.

Clarke, RitaLou, *Pastoral Care of Battered Women*. Philadelphia: The Westminster Press, 1986.

Conn, Charles Paul, *Mom, Dad and the Church*. Cleveland, Tenn.: Pathway Press, 1989.

Cowles, C. S., *A Woman's Place? Leadership in the Church*. Kansas City: Beacon Hill Press, 1993.

Crabb, Larry Ph.D., *The Marriage Builder*. Grand Rapids: Zondervan Publishing House, 1992.

Crary, David, *Wife Battering*. Associated Press Articles

Davies, Brenda Ph.D., *Affairs of the Heart*. Great Britian: Hodder & Stoughton, 2000.

Dobash, Emerson, *Violence Against Wives: A Case Against the Patriarchy*. Free Press, 1973.

Final Report of Canadian Panel on Violence Against Women. Canada: Ministry of Supply and Services. 1993.

Epstein, Seymour, "The Self Concept in E Staub" (Ed) *Personality: Basic Issues and Current Research*. New York: Prentice Hall, 1981.

Evans, Tony Ph.D., Strengthening *Your Marriage*. Tape Ministry, Dallas, Texas

Fischer, James, God *Said Let There Be Woman*. New York: Alba House, 1979.

Fisher, Helen Ph.D., Anatomy *of Love*, Ballantine Books, USA, 1992.

Fortune, Marie, Keeping *the Faith*. San Francisco: Harper and Row. 1987.

Fortune, Marie, *Is Nothing Sacred*. San Francisco: Harper and Row, 1989.

Gerda Lerner, T*he Creation of Patriarchy*. New York: University Press, 1986.

Harley, Willard F. Fall in Love Stay in Love. Grand Rapids: Baker Publishing, 2001

Heald, Cynthia, Loving *Your Husband,* Nave Press Publications Colorado Springs, 1989.

Hendrix, Harville Ph.D., *Keeping The Love You Find.* New York: Pocket Book, 1992.

Henry, Matthew, *Matthew Henry's Commentary,* Vol. VI. Tappen, N.J.: Fleming H. Revell.

Henry, Matthew. Matthew Henry Study Bible. MA: Hendrickson Publishers, 1997

Herring, Jeff. "Marriage: 4 Kinds of Marriage Mates." 3 Oct. 2006. Web. 10 Jun. 2015

Horsfall, Jan, *The Presence of the Past.* North Sydney: I. M. Allen and Unwin, 1991.

Jacobs, Cindy, *Women of Destiny.* Ventura: Regal Books, 1998.

Jones, Ann, N*ext Time She'll Be Dead.* Boston: Beacon Press, 1994.

Kilgore, Nancy, *A Journey Through Domestic Violence Every Eighteen Seconds* California: Volcano Press, 1992.

Levinson, David, *Family Violence in CrossCultural Perspective.* London: Sage Publication, 1989.

May, Rollo, *Power and Innocence.* New York: Fontana, 1979.

Nolte, Dorothy Law, Rachel Harris, and Jack Canfield, Children *Learn What They Live: Parenting to Inspire Values.* Workman Publishing Company. 1998.

Oden, Thomas, *Crisis Ministries* (p 23) New York: Cross, 1986.

O' Leary, K. Daniel. Physical Aggression Between Spouses: A Social Learning Theory Perspective. In Handbook of Family Violence, p 31-55. 1988

Olthuis, James H., *I Pledge you My Troth*. San Francisco: Harper & Row, 1989.

Peck M. Scott Ph.D., *The Road Less Travelled*. New York: Simon and Schuster, 1978.

Pagelow, Mildred, D. Kalmus and M. A. Strauss, *Womenbattering Victims and Their Experiences*. Beverly Hills Sage References, 1981.

Penner, Clifford L Ph.D. and Joyce J. Penner, M.N., R. N., *Men and Sex*. Nashville: Thomas Nelson TN, 1997.

Prokopchak, Steve and Mary, *Called Together*. Camp Hill: Horizon Books, 1999.

Ruether, Mary, *Beyond God the Father: Toward a Philosophy of Women's Liberation*. Boston: Beacon Press, 1973.

Saiving, Valerie, *The Human Situation: A feminine View*. New York: Harper and Row, 1979.

Segundo, Juan Luis, *The Liberation Theology*. Orbis Books, 1976.

Shahin, Jim, *American Way* Magazine, article, February 2, 1999.

Sheridan, James. Sex Before Marriage Can Hurt Relationship. 12 Mar 2014. Web. 17 Jun 2015

Smalley, Gary, *Making Love Last Forever*. Dallas: Word Publishing, 1996.

Smalley, Gary, *Love Is a Decision*. Word Publishing, Dallas TX USA, 1989.

Stahmann, Robert F. and William J Hiebert, *Premarital and Remarital Counseling*. San Franciso: Jossey-Bass, 1997.

Stanton, Glenn T., *Why Marriage Matters*. Colorado Springs: Pinon Press, 1997.

Staubs, Epstein, *Going to Pieces Without Falling Apart*. Random House, Inc., 1999.

Stibbs, Alan, Search *the Scriptures*. Intervarsity Press, 1984.

Storr, Ann, *Family Violence: An International and Interdisciplinary Study*. Toronto: Butterworth, 1978.

Thomas, Joseph, *Crisis Ministries*. New York: Cross Press, 1986.

Vining, John Kie, W*hen Home Is Where the Hurt Is*. Family Ministries

Walker, Lenore, *The Battered Woman*. New York: Harper and Row, 1979.

www.ingramcontent.com/pod-product-compliance
Lightning Source LLC
Chambersburg PA
CBHW071313110426
42743CB00042B/1519